MAGS:
The People Part Of Prepping

How To
Plan, Build And Organize
A Mutual Assistance Group In A
Survival Situation

Charley Hogwood

Foreword by Dr. Joe Alton
Aka Dr. Bones
Author of
"The Survival Medicine Handbook"

All rights reserved.
ISBN-13: 978-1493517855
ISBN-10: 1493517856

DISCLAIMER

The information given and opinions voiced in this book are for educational and informational purposes only.

Although the author has researched all sources to ensure accuracy and completeness, there is no assumption of responsibility for any errors, omissions or other inconsistencies therein. The author does not assume liability for any harm and/or property damage caused by the use or misuse of any methods, products, instructions or information in this book or any resources cited.

The author encourages the reader to research any and all applicable local, state and/or federal laws, rules and regulations pertaining to any information covered in this book. This book is not a substitute for quality instruction with actual professionals in the field of your choice.

No portion of this book may be reproduced by any electronic, mechanical or other means without the express written permission of the author. Any and all requests for such permission should be sent to info@readygoprep.com.

Copyright © 2013
P.R.E.P. Personal Readiness Education Programs, LLC
Cover art: Amarilis Hernandez

Dedication

To Natalie, she is the reason I look forward to tomorrow and cherish yesterday. I hope she comes to learn from my mistakes, adopts my determination and embraces her gifts, for she has much to show the world

To Courtney, my partner, my guardian angel, my best friend. We wake up in love, spend the day laughing with each other, and then close the day feeling lucky to be together. Most people never get to experience the special thing we share.

Acknowledgments

We would like to sincerely thank Dr. Joe Alton and Nurse Amy for their kindness, friendship and mentoring as we pursue our goals of helping families everywhere prepare for life's disruptions, small and large.

Table of Contents

FOREWORD 7

THE SCOPE OF THIS BOOK 13

WHAT IS A MAG AND WHY DO YOU NEED IT 15
    FINDING THE PERFECT MATCH   16
    IT'S A MARATHON, NOT A SPRINT   17
    TIP: BE A GOOD CANDIDATE   18
    MEETING WITH AN ESTABLISHED GROUP   18
    FINDING OTHER GROUPS AND/OR MEMBERS   19

GROUP STRUCTURE, SIZE, AND THE IMPORTANCE OF LEADERSHIP 23
    THE MULTIPLICATION FACTOR   24
    THE INDEPENDENCE CONFLICT   25
    GROUP FORMAT   26
    EXAMPLES OF POPULAR CURRENT GROUP FORMATS 26
        The Community Group   26
        Battle Buddies   27
        The Survival, or Mutual Assistance Group   27
        Networks   29
        Ad Hoc or Hasty Groups   30
    WHY SIZE MATTERS   30
    GROUP LEADERSHIP STYLES: PROS AND CONS   32
        Leadership Options   33
        Key Qualities of a Leader   34
    THE SINGLE LEADER APPROACH   38
    THE COMMITTEE LEADERSHIP APPROACH   40
        Choosing a Committee Leader   40
    THE CONSENSUS LEADERSHIP APPROACH   43
        But What About a Commune?   44
        But Won't Everyone Pitch In On His or her Own? 44

BUILDING A STRONG FOUNDATION 47
    GIVING THE GROUP A DIRECTION   47
    SETTING GROUP GOALS   48
    MAKING AN ACTION PLAN   51
    THE MISSION STATEMENT   51
        Who Should Write The Statement?   53
        Components Of A Good Mission Statement   54
    ESTABLISHING AN OATH   56
        Tips for Writing an Oath   57
    LAW AND ORDER   58
        The Dangers of a Lawless Society   59

The Constitution	60
Rules and Consequences	62
Safety First and Dealing with Attrition	64

SOCIAL CONFLICT AND THE GROUP 65

Privacy Management	65
Problem Members: The 3 Monthers	66
Problem Members: HOA Syndrome	66
Problem Members: Cliques	67
Synergy and Group Fragmentation	68
But Why Is The Rum Gone?	69
Depression and Group Efficacy	70
Avoid Idleness	72
Tend to the Morale of the People	73
Punishment and Ejection	73
Removal Procedures	76
Ejection and the Local Community	77

PICKING A LOCATION FOR YOUR GROUP 79

The Survival Group	79
The Retreat Group	81
Characteristics of a Good Physical Location	82
Finding the Farm for The Survival Group	83
Location Security	*84*
Food Production	*86*
Water Resources	*87*
Shelter Resources	*88*
Health and Safety	*88*
Energy Resources	*89*
Communication	*89*

ROLES AND RESPONSIBILITIES WITHIN THE GROUP 91

Analyzing Group Skills and Resources To Set Priorities	92
The Importance of *Clearly* Defining Roles and Responsibilities	93
The Normalcy Bias	96
Situational Reports and Analysis	98
Interdependency and Combining Tasks	99
Setting Priorities for Group Tasks	*100*
Group Resources and Support	103
Types of Daily Activities	103
Daily Chores	*103*
Special Projects or Operations	*104*
Training	*104*
Security Operations	*107*

THE TEAM CHARTER	109
Setting Up the Team Mission	*111*
Establishing the Team Makeup and Personnel Roles	*112*
Identifying Conflict Between Members and Roles Within The Team	*112*
Setting Limits	*112*
Team Specific Use of Resources	*113*
Assessing Team Feedback Pre- Mission	*113*
THE DIRECTORY OF SPECIALIZED SKILLS	114
Medically Trained Personnel	*115*
Mechanics and Mechanically Inclined Personnel	*115*
Food Production / Farming / Livestock	*116*
Child and Elderly Care	*116*
Educational Staff	*116*
Blue Collar Skills	*116*
Cooks and Food Preparation Staff	*117*
Hunters and Trappers	*117*
Scavengers	*118*
Seamstresses	*119*
Military and Security Personnel	*119*
Ham Radio/Communications Personnel	*120*
Primitive Survivalist or Homesteaders	*120*
Toolmakers/Engineers/Blacksmiths	*121*
Gunsmiths/Experts in Ammo Reloads	*121*
Self Defense	*121*
Solar/Alternate Energy Experts	*122*
Bee keeping	*122*
GROUP FINANCES	124

TRAINING, TEAM BUILDING AND GROUP PROJECTS 125

GETTING THE KIDS INVOLVED	126
FAMILY ACTIVITIES	127
TEACHING OTHERS	128
GETTING STARTED WITH EXERCISES	128
Team Building Exercises	*129*
Getting To Know Each Other Exercises	*129*
Normalizing Exercises	*130*
Ice Breaking Exercises	*131*
WORKING AS A TEAM:	132
THE CRAWL WALK RUN APPROACH	132
IMPROVING GROUP DYNAMICS	133
MINIMIZING DISRUPTIONS AND RESOLVING CONFLICT	135
REDUCING CONFLICT WHEN ADDING NEW TEAM MEMBERS	138

PLANNING FOR CONTINGENCIES 139
- COMPLETING A HAZARD ANALYSIS — 140
- THE HAZARD TREE EXERCISE — 142
- ALL HAZARDS APPROACH — 145
- THE HYBRID TREE EXERCISE — 146
- TRIGGER POINTS — 148
- HOW TO FORMULATE A PLAN — 150
  - *Formulating The Basic Plan* — *151*
  - *Plan Annexes and Supplements* — *153*
- TYPES OF PLANS TO CONSIDER — 154
  - *"But I'm Bored!"* — *154*

DECISION MAKING 159
- PROBLEM SOLVING – INDIVIDUAL DECISIONS — 159
- PROBLEM SOLVING – GROUP DECISIONS — 160
- DECISION MAKING BY CONSENSUS — 161
- GAP ANALYSIS AND BLIND SPOTS IN YOUR PLANNING — 161
  - *What is a Gap?* — *162*
- WHAT IS A BLIND SPOT? — 163
  - *Physical Blind Spots* — *163*
  - *Blind Spots In a Plan* — *164*
- FATAL FLAWS IN DECISION MAKING — 165
- DETECTING PERSONAL BLIND SPOTS — 166

GROUP ACTIVATION PLANS 167
- WE'LL SEE YOU WHEN YOU GET HERE — 169
- WE ARE COMING FOR YOU — 169
- NAVIGATION AND THE STRIP MAP — 170
  - *Strip Map Example* — *172*
- MODIFY THE ACTIVATION PLAN TO SUIT YOUR GROUP — 173
  - *Sample Levels of Activation* — *173*

COMMUNICATION WITH MEMBERS 177

PLANNING AND HOLDING MEETINGS 181
- HANDLING NO-SHOWS — 182
- CONDUCTING EFFECTIVE MEETINGS — 183
  - *Poor Meeting Characteristics:* — *183*
  - *Effective Meeting Characteristics:* — *184*
- PARTICIPANT ROLES IN A MEETING — 185
- THE MEETING AGENDA — 185

NEW MEMBERSHIP 187
- WOMEN IN THE SURVIVAL GROUP — 189
- INDIVIDUAL V. CENTRALIZED THOUGHT — 191
- THE INDIVIDUAL PERSPECTIVE — 193

FINDING GROUP IDENTITY	194
ESTABLISHING BASELINE REQUIREMENTS FOR NEW MEMBERS	196
Mobility - Another Angle To Consider	198
GOOD CANDIDATES, INADEQUATE SUPPLIES	200
VETTING POTENTIAL CANDIDATES	201
STOLEN VALOR	206
CIVILIAN BACKGROUND CHECKS	207
TRUST BUT VERIFY	207
POTENTIAL PROBLEM: PEOPLE KNOCKING ON THE GATE	208

GETTING THE NEW MEMBER OFF TO A GOOD START 211

RESOURCE DISTRIBUTION IN THE GROUP AND BARTERING SURPLUS 213

SKILLS V. SUPPLIES: WHICH MEMBER IS BETTER?	213
INDIVIDUAL V. COMMUNITY SUPPLIES	214
RULE REFRESHER –	215
STEALING AND COMMUNITY RESOURCES	215
SITUATION 1: THE DIVERSE GROUP	216
SITUATION 2: THE BIG FAMILY	217
SUSTAINABILITY AND THE GROUP	217
SURPLUS SUPPLIES AND BARTERING	218
Bartering Safety Tip	220
THE CHARITY PLAN	221
THE STRAY CAT SYNDROME	221
PROTECTING YOUR INVESTMENT	222

THE GROUP AND THE OUTSIDE WORLD 223

SUBTLE CHANGES IN SOCIETY	223
INSIDERS AND OUTSIDERS	224
BUILDING RELATIONSHIPS AND GATHERING INTEL	225 225
ESTABLISHING MUTUAL AID COMPACTS WITH OTHER GROUPS	226
FRIEND OR FOE?	228
EACH GROUP IS DIFFERENT	228
SAFELY NEGOTIATING WITH OTHERS	229
HAVE A DESIGNATED NEGOTIATOR	230
BE CLEAR WHEN MAKING AGREEMENTS	232
FIND COMMON GROUND	233
TRAINING COMPACTS	234

RECOGNIZING AND DEALING WITH OUTSIDE THREATS 235

PEOPLE WILL ALWAYS BE YOUR BIGGEST PROBLEM 235

Risk Homeostasis	236
Behavioural Mimicry	238
Mob Mentality	239
The Thin Line Between Good and Evil	241
Moving From a Hardship Society To A Tactical Perimeter	243
Increased Situational Awareness	244
Security Activation At The Retreat	245

MAKING DUE THROUGH BASELINE PREPAREDNESS 247

ABOUT THE AUTHOR 249

APPENDIX A 251
   Glossary   251

APPENDIX B 262
   Rule of Threes For Survival   262

APPENDIX C 263
   Sample Commo Plan   263

APPENDIX D 266
   Decision Making / Problem Solving Process 266

APPENDIX E 267
   Quick Reference Guide: Forming a Group   267

APPENDIX F 269
   Quick Reference Guide: 269
   Picking a Survival Location In A Hurry   269

APPENDIX E 271
   Reference materials   271

NOTES 285

NOTES 288

NOTES 289

NOTES 290

NOTES 291

NOTES 292

NOTES 293

NOTES 294

NOTES 295

FOREWORD

BY JOE ALTON, M.D. aka Dr. Bones
Author of "The Survival Medicine Handbook"

The decision to adopt disaster preparedness as a philosophy is usually arrived at privately. At one point or another, a light bulb turns on above your head: Maybe it's a good idea to start accumulating supplies to assure your continued success if, for some reason, everything else fails.

Firstly, congratulations! You have become a member of a worldwide community that, while a small percentage of the total population, will have the best chance of surviving a major catastrophe and rebuild society. That community, however, is far-flung and fragmented. You'll need to figure out a way to network locally with like-minded folks to put together what I sometimes call a "village": A set of people with differing skills and knowledge that can help each other in times of trouble. An individual may survive, but it takes a village to thrive.

In one of my lectures, I use a slide that I call "The first thing you'll need to stay healthy in a survival scenario". The slide is a black and white photo of a forlorn-looking creature known as a Tasmanian Wolf. If I wanted a picture of a wolf, why not pick a magnificent red or gray wolf? Simply, because the Tasmanian Wolf is extinct, and so will you be, if you don't have enough people cooperating to perform the activities of daily survival.

So the first thing you'll need to stay healthy is a community. The concept of community is as old as time itself, but few rugged individualists realize its absolute necessity. Without it, even the most prepared person will do little more than eke out a miserable existence.

So how to put together that group of like-minded folks? Very few books address this subject, and this is why I was glad to see that Charley Hogwood has finally decided to put his extensive knowledge of the subject in print. I have known Charley Hogwood for many years now. His list of accomplishments is extensive and I have been impressed with his efforts to put together local mutual assistance groups. At last, here is useful information, in plain English, on how to exponentially increase your chances of survival after a major calamity.

Charley doesn't put out a manifesto of "Do it my way, or you won't make it". There are many ways to skin the proverbial cat, and there are many ways to put together and manage a mutual assistance group. He doesn't necessarily guarantee that this is an easy road to travel. He does, however, give you several reasonable strategies that will help you organize.

No other book has devoted itself to this important issue. In this book, you'll find every factor involved in putting together a successful group discussed in detail. From picking a location to setting up rules to dealing with conflict, Charley Hogwood explains it all for you.

Without realizing it, Mr. Hogwood has even put together a new community by writing this book: Those that realize the importance of working together to work for the common good. This community will be a diverse lot, but will have one thing in common. They'll have this book in their survival library.

Joe Alton, M.D. aka Dr. Bones

Joe Alton is a medical doctor and medical preparedness expert who is the co-author of the #1 Amazon bestseller in Survival Skills and Safety/First Aid, "The Survival Medicine Handbook".

His website at **www.doomandbloom.net** has over 400 articles on disaster preparedness, medicinal gardening, and survival medicine.

Survival MEDICAL Supplies

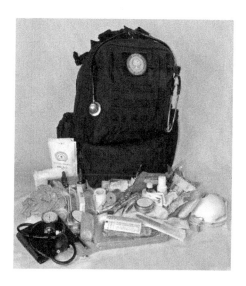

Trauma kits, wound closure kits, herbal meds
Hunter/hiker/biker kits, dental kits, DVDs

And our #1 amazon bestseller
The Survival Medicine Handbook™

By Joe Alton, M.D. and Amy Alton, A.R.N.P.
Aka Dr. Bones and Nurse Amy

Check out our products at:
Store.doomandbloom.net
Your #1 medical preparedness resource

The Scope of This Book

This book is intended for use in several different ways.

First and foremost it is a guide for the survivor to begin his or her journey from solo survivor to established team member. Most people have little idea where or how to start when it comes to finding people to safely connect with. We have established a sequence of actions whereby the novice will be able to accomplish this task with a step-by-step decision-making program. Safety and personal security are constantly running themes throughout the following chapters. Be sure to employ both accordingly.

From our experience we have seen many people get so excited to find people that think similar to them that both sides make poor choices. Sometimes these choices can lead to disastrous and unsafe conditions. This book is designed to service as a guide to help correct those poor choices and the relationships that went with them.

The well-established group should also find this book useful to fine tune their group dynamics and get their teams running smoothly. We address the forces of personnel conflict that cause can render a team completely dysfunctional and offer many strategies to get them back on track. As groups are always looking to prevent turnover and find quality members, we have prepared a long chapter on how to do this with the least amount of risk while still attracting the best candidates to join the ranks.

Finally, this book will serve as a reference guide for on the spot problem solving, addressing everything from admitting members to ejecting members, from setting up an emergency base camp to long-term farm operations. There is no doomsday or conspiracy talk, just proven, actionable knowledge learned from years of hands-on dirty work.

We are keenly aware that many of the concepts, even though proven to work, will be a challenge to implement. We understand that you will not always have a choice in the hand you were dealt and will have to make due with what you have. Even if there are only two of you, the methods in this text will be worth the weight in your backpack.

This book is designed for both today and tomorrow. Post disaster, communities will need to form and people will band together as they have since the dawn of time. Educate yourself and be ready to take charge. Survival is a dirty, hands-on experience that will be much easier if you have some help.

Chapter 1

WHAT IS A MAG AND WHY DO YOU NEED IT

"Take the first step, and your mind will mobilize all its forces to your aid. But the first essential is that you begin. Once the battle is startled, all that is within and without you will come to your assistance."

Robert Collier

So you've thought about it long enough. You understand that there is just no practical way to go it alone or with a small family if a major event hits and your world is turned upside down. A **Mutual Assistance Group** is a group of like-minded individuals who pledge to assist each other in times of crisis. The idea is that many hands make light work. It may or may not be in your best interest to be aligned with one and there are several important things to consider before joining/starting one.

Perhaps you have an interest in starting your own survival group with the preference of building it according to your own set of values. Maybe you'd like to find a group already in existence that has a spot open for your particular skillset. Before you get too far into your search, there are some things you'll want to keep in mind to save yourself a lot of grief and misery down the trail.

Finding the Perfect Match

First, decide what you want from this endeavor. You may begin to notice that much of this process involves soul searching and there is a reason for it. It goes back to why we prepare. The answer is almost always that we are driven to protect ourselves and loved ones in times of trouble. We take the job as protectors of our families very seriously and won't let anything or anyone get in the way of that duty. This is a journey of relationships. Seeking out people with whom we trust the lives of our family is a task not to be taken lightly.

Think of it as marriage with a survival twist. In this case, if it goes bad the spurned lover (and possibly his or her friends) might *actually* take all of your stuff.

To decide if a group is right for you, take some time to answer these questions. Be honest with yourself, and think about your family's answers to these questions as well.

1. Do I work well with others under austere conditions?
2. Will I participate regularly with others to build the group before the SHTF?
3. Is everyone in my family on board with teaming up with others?
4. Will I stay with the group or evacuate under differing scenarios?

If you answered "no" to any of the above questions, you may not be ready to join a group. Keep in mind that the other members are going to depend on you if the time comes.

You will need to participate and contribute regularly to build teamwork and confidence among the members. Often these groups fall apart under their own weight, the thrill diminishes, conflicts of personality arise and people just get busy with other things in life. The last thing anyone needs in the face of crisis is more drama so choose carefully.

It's a Marathon, Not a Sprint
Too often people are so eager to join a group they ignore their gut instincts and think that any obvious conflicts of interest will fade away and everyone will pull together when times are tough.

Here is an example of something that we've run into time and time again when we talk to people about survival groups. Mr. and Mrs. Prepper start to search for like-minded people in their neighborhood, at work and online. They start to feel outnumbered by the unprepared population and become worried that they won't be able to fend off the ill prepared masses when the SHTF (Stuff Hits The Fan). Then it happens, they find someone who has a similar interest and they eagerly hitch their wagons together.

As with all new relationships, or even new employment for that matter, about a month on they start to notice the quirks. At first Mr. and Mrs. Prepper try to justify and ignore the problems as growing pains, hoping everything will work itself out in time. Trust me that time rarely comes. Things don't get better in stressful situations, they get worse. So if you aren't able to find some synergy in everyday pre-collapse life with your group, it won't be better when everyone is in the psychological abyss of a systemic collapse. You get about three days of Kumbaya around the campfire before the unstable people begin to unravel.

While there may be such a thing as love at first sight, it is rare and often too good to be true. Take the time to invest in these relationships, and don't succumb to pressure. If the other people are sincere in their interest in you they will understand and do the same.

Tip: Be a Good Candidate

To be a strong candidate you will need to offer something useful to the group. Some people think they can just buy their way into a group by way of money and equipment then just bask in the protections of others while having no discernible skills. This is a recipe for disaster. One should have something useful by way of a specialty skill that would benefit the group as a whole. You will see many options for skills that will make you a good candidate as we discuss roles and responsibilities. You should also plan to bring as much in the way of supplies as possible.

No one wants to share their hard earned food and medical stores with some new guy who showed up hungry and offers no skills.

It is also important to note that if all you know is security, you are just another mouth to feed. If a group is struggling to feed its members you will not be as attractive a candidate to them. Make an effort to be knowledgeable in something else useful because by the very mission of the group, everyone is a soldier to some extent.

Meeting With An Established Group

So what should you look for when you interview with an established group? It is important to keep in mind the reason for this journey is to have help in case of disaster or troubled times.

These are potentially people you will need to live with and possibly fight along side under the toughest conditions. It pays to make sure they embrace the same values, ethics, views and goals as you. This is a tall order but it's a good place to start. Before you commit to anything attempt to participate in some of their meetings or team building events and try to meet as many members as possible. The reason for this is to get an overall feel for how things work, who is in charge and what personalities stand out. Once you become comfortable, slowly ease in and show your willingness to participate as an equal by offering your skills and knowledge at events.

Remember, at this point you are courting the group and they are trying to decide if you will be allowed to stay. Follow your instincts and decide whether these people are a good fit for you.

In a case of instant disaster you may need to make judgment calls as to whether you should link up with whoever comes along but all the same rules apply and use your best judgment based on whatever information you have available. It is survival after all, and you do what you can, when you can.

Finding Other Groups and/or Members

This is the million-dollar question for almost everyone we've ever met. Keep your eyes and ears open at all times but begin close to home, as that's where you are likely to need the most help. If you have a retreat location, you'll want to make sure you put the time in in that community. Just because you have property in some small town doesn't mean the people there will welcome you if they don't know you. Unfortunately far too many misinformed preppers are under the impression that they are just going to bug-out to "the hills" or "the woods". I can assure you that the people that live in those hills, and around those woods, don't want anything to do with you.

When looking for similarly minded people to partner with there are plenty of options available. In some cases groups might be aware of you before you even know they exist. Some groups use a funneling system to meet potential candidates. It's not as nefarious as it sounds. It just means that members who are survival minded tend to frequent or operate businesses or locations that other survival minded people might also frequent. If they see someone who might be a good candidate, they'll talk to them. So, keep your mind open. The next time someone strikes up a conversation about the world today, they may be sizing you up. In the meantime, here are some potential meeting places (both online and in person):

- Join a CERT (Community Emergency Response Team) Team or other community group.
- Frequent a local farmers market.
- Take classes in skills such as gardening or bee keeping.
- Take some primitive survival classes such as fire starting or water purification.
- Learn target or tactical shooting or join a hunting club.
- Join an active local online meetup.com group that hosts activities related to self reliance/survival.
- Make friends at church and other community events.
- Volunteer with your local emergency services or at the Emergency Operations Center (EOC)

Remember, this book can be used as a guide to start a group from scratch or as a reference book to put a sharper edge on an existing team. We are keenly aware that many of the concepts, even though proven to work, will be hard to implement.

However, by carefully planning ahead, you can hopefully prevent chaos later on when times may not be as good. This group will become your new extended family, so take the time now to make sure that you're ready to go when the proverbial stuff hits the fan.

NOTES:

Chapter 2

GROUP STRUCTURE, SIZE, AND THE IMPORTANCE OF LEADERSHIP

"When the best leader's work is done the people say 'We did it ourselves.'

Lao Tzu

The MAG/Survival Group is just like any other organization. It doesn't matter what form you decide on, every group will need some version of leadership and some form of arrangement or organization if it is to be at the ready when disaster strikes. Some smaller groups prefer to operate with only with a general understanding of each other's goals and rely on the argument that safety in numbers is enough. When you have a couple of friends that understand each other, this theory may work. However, it is when the numbers grow that chaos can reign. What many people fail to realize is how fast the numbers can add up.

Let's say that three friends decide to work together and form a survival group. At this point they already know why but maybe not how so they start talking to family and friends. If each member has the average family of 1 spouse, 2 children and perhaps a set of grandparents, this means that the three-person group could already number 12 people. That was fast. Another consideration would be additional incoming friends, family or neighbors that would be difficult to turn away in a crisis. Needless to say, what started out as 3 buddies who pledged to form a group has potentially evolved into 25+ members.

The Multiplication Factor

This is a good point in our discussion to stop and consider some group dynamics. You know why you are seeking to join or establish a group and are comfortable in your decision. What about your spouse, children (young or older), or others that you wouldn't leave behind? What are the ramifications of essentially dumping so many personalities into a survival situation, alongside total strangers, under stressful conditions, in what may be cramped lodging? We know statistically that many of the "follow on" crowd will not be skilled or have sufficient supplies to sustain themselves. They may not be interested and may even resist altogether. This will have to be planned for.

Often we hear people state that they will only show up with their pre-planned number of approved members and will have no problem leaving some family behind. This statement by itself should send alarm bells to you about how they are prepared to walk away when times are tough. Regardless, the fact is that you cannot count on such statements and a fudge factor must be built in. A factor of +/-10% is reasonable to account for changes in final group numbers when the group is actually activated post-disaster.

Why is the percentage plus *or* minus? Because even though everyone says they will show up, invariably some won't. When it comes down to it, some may not survive, may be delayed for long periods or just decide to shelter in place because they can't leave the relative safety of home and family.

Additionally, some people just won't be able to leave Aunt Mabel and Uncle Morty (or Neighbor Jane or Cousin Billy or whomever) when the time comes. This is the reality in a long-term survival group situation and must be considered in advance when planning for decision maker positions, lodging and resources.

The Independence Conflict

In our experience working with groups we have heard plenty of stories and theories on how to operate groups and in some cases, communes. Many people can appreciate the benefits of belonging to a group but many aren't ready to hand over their personal sovereignty to be led by another. Preppers are by nature leaders and tend to want to be in control. The sheer fact that you are making the decision to be less dependent on the "system" says that you don't trust that someone will be there to save you when the chips are down.

The same struggle will happen within a group. After all, if you don't want to depend on the government or anyone else to be there in hard times, why should you relinquish some of your independence to other people just because you are in a group? We'll call this the *Independence Conflict* for our discussion. So how can we overcome this obvious conflict of interest? The short answer is through reflection and self-preparedness. You'll need to decide what you are willing to trade for the safety and security of a group. As with any endeavor, the more you bring to the table, the better your position. This doesn't mean just supplies, but includes personal skills and the ability to improve the overall health of the group.

Group Format

Groups are formatted in several ways. We are going to operate under the assumption that you are working with a blank slate and have the opportunity to design your group from the ground up. If you are already involved with others in some organized fashion, perhaps you will pick up some ideas to resolve current conflict or enhance your group efficiency and readiness.

Examples of Popular Current Group Formats

The Community Group

They live near enough to help each other in case of localized emergencies. Usually, these members are close enough to each other that if there are travel restrictions established by authorities they wouldn't be considered outsiders thus prevented from neighborhood access.

What are potential travel restrictions? Often during an emergency event, only people with approved business are allowed into the affected area. If a resident has been evacuated or caught outside the perimeter, he or she may not be allowed in until law enforcement has deemed the area safe. This could be many hours, days or possibly weeks. Neighbors would fall into this category.

The community group usually communicates with each other through social media or in person and even gets together as friends in social situations. They may have a community agreement to help each other in case of emergency. They may or may not actively plan or practice for an activation, but claim to be there for each other.

There will be no real leadership but there will be those who are more active in the local community and as such are considered organizers. During peacetime most members will not appreciate strict leadership and are too busy in their daily lives to actively build and practice an emergency plan. There will be challenges for authority, possible fragmentation and those who choose to keep to themselves in the neighborhood unless something important calls them into service.

Groups such as this run rampant with rumor and bandwagon mentality. It is for this reason that we will include online forums and social media groups.

Battle Buddies

They are usually nearby neighbors, friends or family who form an alliance to take care of each other in times of need. BBs may also be a group within a group on a more personal level, such as brothers, best friends, etc. They may have specific plans to work together in advance of an emergency, and may build inventory and supplies together, possibly even practice skills.

Sometimes family that arrives can fall into this category but this is generally a very small team. There will usually be a natural leader based on personality and skill set for the given scenario.

The Survival, or Mutual Assistance Group

As we talked about earlier, a mutual assistance group is an organized, like-minded group of individuals and/or families that seek each other out to form a self-reliant community arrangement with each other. Group members may move in or around each other or plan to meet in case of a situation that requires activation of their plan.

The group regularly gathers to plan, educate, practice skills and train for predetermined scenarios. This group is usually tight knit and vets new members carefully knowing that their security is at stake should they choose wrong with future candidates. These groups have various personnel arrangements to meet stated goals.

Some of these arrangements are as follows:

MAGS: The Live-Ins

The Live-Ins will usually have a farm, retreat or home location where some members live year-round tending to crops and livestock. They keep the retreat at a high level of readiness at all times so that if activated, incoming members will have a place to go.

They live a life of sustainability and self-reliance, their version of "practice what you preach". In some instances the retreat members cultivate relationships, mutual assistance and barter agreements with local business and law enforcement in an effort to receive Intel of interest within the community. They may or may not advertise their intentions to the community at large depending on the determined mission statement. Note that it may be difficult to keep such an operation confidential in a small town.

MAGS: The Live-Outs

These are members who are usually associated with a retreat location that may or may not be manned regularly. They are usually people who have regular jobs somewhere else and may live in another town.

They will make plans to go to the retreat location any number of times per year to perform maintenance, take turns working the crops or train on skills. Many will use their vacation time to visit the retreat. In case of activation, they will "Bug-Out" to the retreat and settle in for the duration of the event

MAGS: The Hybrids or Independents

These are associates of a group that support the group from outside of a retreat location through mutual assistance. They may wish to keep their independence but still have options in case the situation worsens to the point where they wish to "come inside".

These may also be individuals in a community or neighborhood who participate in security and reactionary efforts such as repelling attacks or fire fighting but not other group activities such as gardening or assisting the vulnerable.

Networks

These are loosely organized, usually leaderless frameworks that will support individuals or families of the organization who may need assistance or temporary lodging in case of disaster. Part of the framework will usually include contingency plans available to all members who will then download and print for use in case of a total grid down scenario.

Every member will be aware of activation levels, marking techniques and possibly neighboring members. This will form a web of safety for evacuation in every direction should the situation require evacuation. Assistance requests are predetermined and volunteers usually self deploy to make contact with the nearest members in case of disasters, such as tornados or earthquakes to check on the affected members.

Nationwide networks will have predetermined plans to move needed supplies into a disaster area in small containers such as pods and usually only to specifically registered members. Members may become a sort of Underground Railroad to move personnel and material to their destinations.

Ad Hoc or Hasty Groups

Usually formed out of necessity in a crisis (such as a major earthquake or other no-notice event) where strangers may come together out of a natural desire to work together. There is little vetting of members, if any, and often there are very few materials or an unbalanced inventory of supplies on hand at the outset.

Examples include survivors trapped in a building, a group lost in the wilderness or victims of a crash or sinking ship. In extreme cases or longer-term scenarios, members will begin to leave the group to find their way home and others may arrive looking for help making longer-term survival more of a challenge with an unstable skill base and personality and leadership differences.

Did you see a scenario that resembled your situation in the above examples? You probably noticed that there are pros and cons to each format. By observing the different formats you should be able to choose wisely the kind of group you want to organize. At any rate, it all goes back to what it is you are personally looking for in a group.

Why Size Matters

The size of the group is an important consideration, and has particular consequences as it increases over a certain number. A British anthropologist named Robin Dunbar studied primates and their relationships.

His work revealed that the traditional effective limit of any group is about 150 members. Professor Dunbar, after years of research, noted that when a group reached approximately 150 members, the individuals began to lose the ability to maintain close relationships. Interestingly, military units, tribes, villages, small businesses and other small organizations naturally lose effectiveness around this point. 150 members is the average size of a military troop or company size element going back to the Roman Empire.

There are several other sociological limits before this number. For example, let's take a look at some common group sizes:

Two people can be very creative (as observed by any parent who's made the mistake of leaving 2 toddlers unattended) but lack the resources for complete survival and would be working to diminishing returns over time. Also, any injury or incapacitation would put extreme pressure on the healthy partner, as they would now be responsible for assisting both rehabilitation, as well as everyday survival tasks.

Three people could become unstable with one person feeling left out, or #3 would be a controlling vote when opinions are split during decision making. Incidentally, this could lead to another member feeling left out, increasing tension and animosity. This can be especially exacerbating if it is a couple and a single person attempting to work together.

Four people will often split into pairs, which can lead to animosity and/or secrecy.

Five to eight people are really the beginning of a team, and allows for multiple tasks to be completed simultaneously. With this type of structure, 8 people is about the limit where everyone will openly participate in discussions and feel as if they have any say with respect to direction and health of the group.

With numbers **between 9 and 12**, you have the introduction of background noise and meetings become boring or too long. At this level members will begin to feel as if they are not receiving enough attention or will become lost in the crowd, especially if there are stronger personalities that tend to dominate discussions.

There are large survival groups in existence but they usually require a diverse leadership structure to efficiently manage the resources and collective tasks needed to provide for so many members. Some groups are in the 200-member range but require strict organization to be sustainable and self-reliant. They also become hybridized in their operations where they rotate live-in and live-out members through the retreat location to supplement the labor force and keep members trained in various skills.

Group Leadership Styles: Pros and Cons

"Leadership has never been about the rank or position you hold. It's about the example you set"
Keni Thomas
Ranger in the "Blackhawk Down" Mission

No matter the group makeup, there must be leadership. Just as true democracy is anarchy, so is a group without some form of structure. Throughout the ages man has struggled with independence versus authority.

A quick look at the world today will show the various forms of government, and the daily struggle between citizens and authority.

It is notable that no nation exists successfully under absolute democracy, certainly none of the advanced nations. A lesson can be learned from the most efficient organizations. Whether they are corporate or military, these types of organization have something in common; they understand that it is *absolutely necessary* to have a command structure in place.

For instance, a corporation requires teamwork and management to achieve goals in everything from sales to production to delivery of the product. Without it, the business will implode under the weight of mismanagement, cease to exist and be ripe for hostile takeover.

The military at all unit levels must display discipline, teamwork and communication in order to successfully conduct any mission. In the case of the military, lives will depend on these requirements. This is not to say your group should be run as a top-heavy industrial conglomerate or a well oiled unit of killers, but there must be authority to achieve legitimacy.

Note that without legitimacy, authority will not be respected. Then, without authority, discipline will falter. Finally, without discipline there can be no unified direction. This is why deciding on a leadership structure is paramount to group success.

Leadership Options

There are several common options available to groups that don't require the re-inventing of the proverbial wheel. These structures may stand independently or be merged to create the final product.

- Single Leader
- Committee / Task Leadership
- Consensus by Vote

We touched on the conflict regarding independence vs. authority earlier. When you put any number of strong personalities in a group there will be animosity. Conversely, indecisive members may delay needed decisions. To not decide is still a decision but may not enhance your situation and shows weakness. The old command of "right or wrong, make a decision" still applies and should be emphasized by group leaders.

To make matters worse, imagine these personalities trying to navigate a world without law and few basic resources. The scenario sounds pretty scary, especially if you have ever seen a heated parents and teachers meeting at an elementary school. This is why it's so important to have strong leadership from the very beginning of this journey.

Whichever structure you choose, it must be documented and its authority must be accepted to obtain legitimacy. It doesn't matter whether you have ten members or one hundred members, in order to maintain effectiveness your group must all be on board or when things get tough, there will be problems.

Key Qualities of a Leader

Whatever leadership structure is chosen for the group, it's important to make sure that the leader(s) possess strong leadership skills. What are essential leadership skills? There is no way to include all the hard learned lessons and nuances a leader must be able to apply in this text, or the book would be over 1000 pages. The best we can offer for a reference are some characteristics of strong leaders, someone that can motivate people in times of peace so that they may follow in times of peril.

To be an effective leader you must be willing to constantly work to improve yourself. No one is born a natural leader that never needs to improve. Since becoming a good leader is a lifetime endeavor, one must observe others who demonstrate the skills that motivate people to follow. Pick good role models and practice their techniques. Learn from your mistakes and don't be afraid to admit them. Strong leaders will focus on finding strengths within themselves and others.

We all have more weaknesses than strengths. Rather than try to compensate for weakness, make every effort to improve your strengths. Building a team is about filling in the gaps, for instance where you may be weak, another may be strong. Combine those strengths and you will become a formidable force.

The weaknesses will become less of a liability and every member will become an equal part of the group, which will in turn improve morale and commitment.

The leader will at all times *act as if someone is watching*. The leader understands that as he or she becomes more effective, he or she becomes a role model to others, just as he or she chose his role models. It is said that the words from those we love hit harder than from a stranger. For this reason the leader will want to choose words carefully. Your job is to lead and mentor and your words can make or break those who look up to you. Use praise whenever possible to encourage good work but don't be sarcastic, be sincere. Your negativity towards someone is also amplified. Be careful to not demean or belittle those who look to you for answers. Instead, help them find their way.

A leader must absolutely *demonstrate integrity*. When people trust that you have their best interests at heart, will be there for them, and will live up to your word, they will be open to follow you.

Trust is difficult to earn. It is essential that you trust those who you report to in order to perform to the best of your ability, *and* that they trust you to make good decisions for the group as a whole. People need to trust that you always have their best interest in mind.

As a leader you must also *inspire people to act.* How do you do this? Offer a vision of what the future will hold if everyone pulls together. Keep promoting the vision and use measurable goals and milestones to show that if everyone works together and puts in their best efforts, the vision can be achieved. Be sure to remain optimistic even in the worst of times. People are looking up to you. If you become negative so will everyone else.

In order for people to accomplish a task they will need support in several ways. There is nothing worse than being asked to do something and get no help or tools to get it done. If the team hits a wall in some way that they cannot overcome, the leader should be there to help them by offering extra resources or clearing the way.

There's an old saying in the Army, *"The message that might be misunderstood will be misunderstood."* What does this mean for the leader? It means that proper and effective communication is key to leading a successful group. Once you have effectively communicated the task at hand, have confidence that it can be done. Make sure the team knows that failure is not an option, and you know it is possible through their efforts. If you are not confident, the team won't be either.

Communication is both written and verbal, and a good leader is effective at both. It has been said that it is not good enough to communicate so that you are understood, you must communicate in a manner that you are not misunderstood.

This follows the keep it simple method. Be clear; remove any ambiguity from your orders. Use reflective listening and brief back to be sure every one understands what is expected of them. Keep channels open by encouraging communication at all levels, both up the chain of command and down.

A strong leader leads by example. You must show that you won't ask others to do something you aren't willing to do yourself. Conversely, if someone isn't willing to do what you are, can they be trusted to get the job done when you aren't looking? If a subordinate leader refuses to get dirty along side of you, how will he be able to lead others? People will watch the interaction of two leaders if they see regular disagreement, it will eventually cause distrust.

Be decisive, you are a leader because you have demonstrated the ability to make good decisions. Don't be afraid to make tough decisions quickly when you need to. As long as you err on the side of the group goals you will have likely decided correctly. Once you have decided on something, stick with it unless something compels you otherwise. Just be sure to gather as much information as the decision requires before you commit to something big.

When partnering with an outside group you must remember that trust isn't built between groups, it is built between people. Harvest relationships between people and groups will more effectively work together. When there is a lack of trust, groups are always positioning to preserve their own interests.

Remember that there is no one person that embodies absolutely all of the traits that we just mentioned. However, these paragraphs should give you an idea of the kind of person you would want in charge of your group.

If you're building your own group, who best fits this description? Be honest, it may not be you.

If you're joining a group, ask yourself if their leader has some of these traits. Hint: Just because someone has "led groups" before, doesn't mean that they are a good leader and should automatically be in charge. Take time to learn about the group's leadership structure, and see if you would be happy working both under and alongside the individuals in charge. This is another time to be honest with yourself and determine whether the person, or persons, in charge are deserving of those positions.

Now, let's move on to the pros and cons of different leadership styles for the MAG.

The Single Leader Approach

"Fate, or some mysterious force, can put the finger on you or me, for no reason at all."
Martin Goldsmith

What are some of the benefits to having a single leader? Though it brings up images of kings and tyrants, there is something to be said about having one point of contact and having one person as the main decision maker. It allows for quick decisions when necessary, and prevents some of the bureaucracy associated with the consensus and/or committee approach.

A single leader group may be effective in small numbers, but if the group increases in size the leader will experience problems with what is called a *Span of Control*. Span of control refers to the relationship between a leader and subordinates, and is designed to keep the leader effective.

An effective ratio of subordinates is between 3 and 7 workers to one leader depending on the complexity of a task and the competence of the individuals. The ideal ratio is 1 leader, 5 subordinates. When you have a span of control that's larger, for instance 1 leader and 15 subordinates, you can see how difficult it becomes to keep everyone in line. Ask any kindergarten teacher with 30 students and they would definitely agree with this.

The reason I bring this up is to demonstrate how ineffective it would be to have one leader for a large group, especially when the group is tasked with many daily objectives.

This also correlates with the independence conflict we discussed earlier, where many members are not interested in having someone else tell them what to do.

Also, if this is a long time group of friends that have always been about equal in status, the recently promoted group leader may find that being advanced to a leadership position among his peers might bring power base problems. Why? Because friends may be unable to respect the leader now that he is in charge. For this reason it is sometimes beneficial to bring a leader in from a different department or group to maintain a separation between leader and followers. This is why fraternization between officers and enlisted is a bad thing in the military.

In critical fields such as security and tactical operations it is very important to maintain discipline and promote effective teamwork. Power base problems are not limited to single leader organizations but can happen in any collective task where someone must take the lead or make decisions.

The Committee Leadership Approach

Committee Leadership (also called Council Leadership) groups are effective when there are enough members to round out the many tasks of daily survival. In a later chapter we will dive into the different types of tasking required in support of your group. The idea behind a committee is to give each major task a seat at the table for decision-making. For instance, food production, security and medical groups should all be represented in the committee.

Committees usually operate under a vote system whereby each task leader acts as a cabinet member and either advises the group leader or in the case of no group leader, the different committee heads will vote by majority on pending decisions.

Some groups prefer to avoid titles and will instead have just a gentleman's understanding of who is a voting member and who is not.

Depending on the size of the overall group, there may be any number of people who work under or along side of the committee head. An example would be farming/gardening, where there may be one person in charge of the farming committee, and then multiple members working on individual farming chores. As the group size increases, the number of people assigned to the task increases. The farm and garden group will need a voice to communicate their needs and food yields.

Choosing a Committee Leader

A good strategy would be to appoint the highest qualified person as the primary committee member and next highest qualified person (not related to, or traveling with the primary) to the alternate position.

You must use care in appointing both the primary committee leader and the alternate committee leader.

First of all, there should be redundancy in positions *if at all possible*. The reason for redundancy is that in the very likely scenario where someone does not show up for activation, or in a disaster situation, someone else who is similarly qualified can fill in.

A particularly volatile situation can arise when two members of the same family desire to be primary and alternate leaders of a specific task group. For instance, what if there is a husband and wife who both want to head up a critical skill group.

A critical skill would be anything that requires experience or specialized training above a layman's knowledge, potentially including committees for gardening, medical, tactical, etc.

This is not to say they can't both serve in the same department, just that they should not hold simultaneous leadership in the same department or committee level leadership in separate departments.

Why is this a problem? Because even though both members are well qualified and would be a tremendous asset to the group in that capacity, a loss could present serious problems that affect the entire group. What will the group do if something prevents the couple from reaching the group? They could be victims of the disaster, injured along the way, delayed, lost, or just choose to not come at all. What if, pre-disaster, they both quit the group? This leaves the entire group vulnerable.

Another problem that can present itself is if multiple members of the same family hold key voting positions at the table. In a vote for majority decision, family may swing the vote. For example, let's say that there is a four-person committee, two are husband and wife, how do you think a difficult vote might turn out? What about a five-person committee?

Who is going to be in the unfortunate position to be the tiebreaker and possibly alienate two entire departments? If the two related members get mad and leave, you are back to being down in 2 departments.

If this is allowed to happen, the group just lost out on important people, which could collapse the whole department or even the group as a whole. Not to mention the effect on morale the arguing will have. It is also important to note that no single member should be so important to the group that if they were lost, the group would fail.
Groups should be organized in such a way that be it ejection or death of a member, the group moves on intact. By preventing two close members from holding the same committee position you should be able to mitigate the potential problem.

It is my opinion that only one person from a close family be allowed a committee voting right. This doesn't apply to a group wide vote, just inner circle leadership. Again, *if at all possible*. The Committee Leadership approach works best in mid-large size groups, where there are ample members to form committees and perform the necessary tasks. For instance, if you have a group of only 6 people, the single leader, or consensus approach may be better suited for your group.

The Constitutional Group

Though largely similar to the Committee Leadership approach, there are certain well-established groups who operate with the belief that there should never be a security element that controls the group.

This is more in line with a Constitutional way of thinking and aims to employ a separation of power among the leadership council.

These groups believe that power corrupts the individual, and power when there are weapons involved is not a healthy combination for free society to flourish. They choose to be the protectors of their community, only called into action in times of need.

The group will usually stay on the sidelines ready to work until called upon or needed. They prefer to have a close relationship with a Constitutional Sheriff and not be viewed as outlaws so they may assist in a time of need.

Note that a relationship with the Sheriff can vary wildly depending on how the Sheriff feels about the 2nd Amendment.

If there is a civic government still in existence in a community, the Constitutional Group will provide protection for the Mayor and City Council so that they can tend to needs of the citizens. Following a similar path is also a religious survival group. If your group is operated and organized by the Church, church leadership will likely be the governing body.

The Consensus Leadership Approach

Consensus Leadership is sometimes suggested as a solution to overcome the independence conflict. In reality, consensus is never leadership. That's not to say there isn't a place for a group vote. What the larger size group may find is that without clear leadership there will be electioneering or disagreement that cannot be overcome due to stronger personalities. An additional problem with consensus leadership is that it is time consuming and potentially leaves a large group of people feeling unsatisfied about decisions made for the benefit of the group. If an entire minority section of the group feels that their needs are not being met and that the majority is pushing them around. That tension will only hinder the group's progress overall.

Regardless of size, some groups may find that a visible majority vote by raised hand or anonymous written ballot will show the division and popularity of a decision. If secret ballots are used they should be verified in public by a selected ballot chairperson and witnessed by all members or section leaders. Raised hand votes should be yea or nay.

But What About a Commune?

There are those that have claimed that a leaderless commune can work and everyone will work together with no need for any management at all. After exhaustive discussion and investigation, it turns out that there was always some form of leadership within the commune but it was performed with such nuance and subtlety that many didn't understand they were actually being led toward common goals. The leaders of the group were just not labeled as leaders, this giving the appearance that everyone was equal. In some cases, they were "elders" who naturally attracted followers and led by charisma and experience. In other cases, the leaders were other workers who labored alongside their neighbors but carried the weight to speak for their subgroup at meetings and have final say on decisions.

This form of cooperation may work in a peacetime commune of vegan drum circlers. But in a survival situation where bad decisions can risk injury or starvation with the added stress of separated families and the grief of death and dying, people will not be so patient and forgiving.

But Won't Everyone Pitch In On His or her Own?

This is another variation of the theory that "everyone comes together in times of crisis." It has been said that in an extreme disaster all the members will come together and work toward the greater good so there would be no need for any real leadership. While there is some truth to this, the concerns here are many.

Division of labor will become a point of contention among group members, as any high school student with a group project will tell you that no one ever volunteers to split the project equally.

What happens if some individuals choose to mentally give up or sham their duties in turn laying burdens on others? It is well known that 20% of any group usually performs 80% of the work. Yes, even in established survival groups.

While the high school student can get over the perceived injustice, in a survival situation this could lead to mutiny and /or group fragmentation if left to fester in the community. For group harmony it is especially important to monitor each person for injury, both physical and psychological lest unknown issues come to a head at the least opportune time.

It is for this reason that we encourage, when possible, groups to implement their leadership structure of choice as early on as possible.

NOTES:

Chapter 3

BUILDING A STRONG FOUNDATION

"If you don't have solid beliefs you cannot build a stable life. Beliefs are like the foundation of a building, and they are the foundation to build your life upon."

Alfred A. Montapert

Many people misinterpret the value of properly organizing. Just as you wouldn't begin building a home without a solid foundation, it is important to do some foundational work to create or reestablish a strong group. Our forefathers understood the value of identifying rights, powers and limitations for a more perfect union. Those documents are just as important to American survival and harmony today as they were well over two hundred years ago.

Giving the Group a Direction

In order for the group to take shape and truly fulfill its mission, you will want to establish some common goals. Sure, you may be able to operate for a while by just getting together every once in a while for a barbecue with your similarly minded friends. If the group spent every meeting eating a potluck dinner and cocktails with little umbrellas, how can they possibly come together as a team to perform all the important duties needed to survive under austere conditions? The socialization aspect is very important and the group should get together as often as possible, but it would be wise to take advantage of every meeting opportunity to do something survival or teamwork related. This is where goals come into play.

Setting Group Goals

What do goals have to do with developing a team? Goals give direction. If you don't know where you want to go, how can you figure out how to get there? Another military reference that translates to the group is "train as you would fight and fight as you have trained." What kind of goals would a survival group want to consider? To answer that question, think back to your own interest in preparedness.

- Why do you prepare?
- What do you do to prepare?
- How do you prepare as a family?
- What kind of things would you like to work on to further your preparedness in the future?
- What have you found in your prepping journey that wasn't helpful?

If you look at a survival group as an extension of your immediate family, it is easier to envision the kinds of goals that would be helpful. We all know how hard it can be to get family to move in one direction, imagine what would happen if a group went about preparing in those same directions. There is also the problem of someone feeling his or her idea is the best idea, every time. By establishing group goals you can mitigate this problem so that all of the group members are getting what they want (at least for the most part) out of the group. Once goals are set, most people will work within the framework of those goals. If they choose to pursue other projects, they will work on them at their own pace. This way, if and when the group desires their ideas, they already have much of the concept and design ready to go.

Once the group has goals, it will use them to decide on how to establish their founding principals. The group goals can be as lofty as you wish, but remember that this is a group designed for a post-disaster world, and the ultimate goal is survival. The group must be prepared to operate in harsh conditions and possibly in a societal situation that members have never before experienced. Bad things may happen and people will change. Later on as we explore the sociological behaviors of such a society, it will become clear why goals are so important.

When considering your goals, think about what is good for the group but also think about you personally. Make sure to think of what you *want* from the group and about what you *do not want* from the group. If you don't set a moral anchor now, a desperate situation later will make it easier to convince yourself to become someone that you don't like or want to be. This is not to say that you can't change if needed in a bad situation, but at least you will have a reference point to return to in the future. Rather than attempt to read your mind and write my interpretation of what your goals may be, here are some general categories. It is not complete as we are all in different situations.

This is a guide to help you get started now and a primer for stressful times. Feel free to add, as you need to fit your conditions.

- *Do you have any set preparedness milestones that you feel are important for your family? For the group? When do you want to reach these milestones?*
- *Are you open to outside members? If so, how many would you like to have?*
- *Do you have a goal of preparing a retreat location?*

- *What period of time should the group have in mind for food storage pre-disaster? Months, years?*
- *Is there a list of skills you would like to acquire? This year? Next?*
- *Would you like to raise a certain amount of money for group projects? Time frame?*
- *Should there be a goal of baseline materials for each member? New members?*
- *Would you like to have a HAM radio set up? When?*
- *Would you like the group to participate in a certain number of overnight events each year?*
- *Would you like to plan events for the meeting schedule? What is the theme for each month's meeting?*

Whatever goals you set, make sure they are high priorities or they may get lost in the chaos. When they are important to you and to the mission, they will more likely remain in focus. Try not to set too many goals, just the ones that make you feel as if "I need this". There is a method to goal setting that helps to make sure what you think is a goal is actually a goal and not an idea.

The **SMART** method helps accomplish this.

- *Specific* – The goal must be clear and well defined
- *Measurable* – Use dates and amounts so you can measure your success
- *Attainable* – Make sure the goal can be achieved
- *Relevant* – The goal should be in line with the direction you want the group to go and its mission
- *Time-Bound* – Set a realistic deadline. This will give a sense of urgency and a better chance to be completed. Open-ended projects always seem to get delayed.

When setting the goals for the group, write them down, record them in the meeting minutes. This way you can refer back to the original intention.

Making an Action Plan

Too often we get so caught up in the goal setting, we forget to figure out how to get there. Get together with the team or assign the task of drawing up a plan with the steps needed to achieve the goal to one particular person. As the steps are completed, cross them off the list so you can see where the project stands at any given time. This offers incentive, and keeps the momentum going as either you personally, or the group as a whole move towards accomplishment.

Keep at it and try not to lose focus. If the project seems to run aground, get it back on the rails and try to figure out what went wrong. The problem is usually too many other things going on, lack of resources or poor management. If the group set this goal as important, is it still important? The goals of the group are like the road map to survival. Get everyone going the same direction and things will get done.

The Mission Statement

The mission statement defines *who* your group is. Consider the mission statement to be the cornerstone of your new home. For our discussion the group will be a general survival-oriented community. In other scenarios, a group may be more aggressively tactical, or restricted to only family, or perhaps has a strictly charitable focus. There are many combinations of how such a group might operate, and this is why it is so important to define who you are and how you would like to operate early on.

Draw upon the goals you established earlier when we discussed giving the group direction. This will help you complete the mission statement. One thing is important here, remain consistent! Take the time to review your goals and documents for continuity. Make sure your message is the same throughout. The group goals are not just an exercise in corporate psychobabble; they are the glue that the group can hold on to when times are tough, they are the message you want to convey to new and potential members. Everyone should understand what the goals are to keep things running smoothly in good times and bad.

In this way, if things get difficult or the group's focus seems to going in different directions, you'll be able to compare the new direction with your original stated goals and mission. This will help to refocus your direction or at least understand that it is time for the discussion of amending the mission through intelligent discourse.

Another potential problem that can be prevented through the use of a mission statement has to do with expectations. When people form personal expectations about something, and those expectations fail to materialize from misunderstanding or poor leadership, disillusion always follows and dissention trails close behind. By creating and promoting clear objectives, you will reduce the pitfalls of imagined expectations.

The chaos and confusion of a grid down event is not the time to make the rules up on the fly, if at all possible. This is not to say you will have it all figured out before the fan sludges to a halt, but the more you do in preparation, the smoother the aftermath will be.

Remember, our goal is to make the best of what may be a very bad situation, but the likelihood of everything being perfect is still very slim. There will be growing pains. Sometimes it will seem as if your group will never work, but structure and unity will eventually win out, especially if everyone believes in what they are doing.

As we delve into building your foundation you will find that these methods will give you something to work toward. Even if you already have a group organized, this groundwork will serve as guidance and reference in a world full of difficult choices.

Who Should Write The Statement?

One member or several members can write the Mission Statement, as long as the statement accurately describes exactly what the goals of the group are. This can be the group's first exercise in finding real common ground. It may turn out to be an eye opener. This and other collective tasks will demonstrate any fractures or misunderstandings very quickly. It is better to find out now before things get tough. If at any time the group gets hung up, back off and ask each other to identify their goals on paper. When this is done collaborate to find common ground.

One thing about the mission statement that is more important than anything else is that everyone in the group completely agrees and "buys into" the final written statement. If there are holdouts, or those that see the mission in different ways it won't matter what is written.
This is exactly why the statement needs to be written in the first place, to make sure everyone clearly understands and supports the group as a whole, and to reduce friction and confusion.

In the survival environment there will be plenty of both to go around. It's best to get a grip on group ideals early on before people with attitudes, guns and few laws begin feuding. Look at the mission statement as the reason you are all here.

For those that cannot come to agreement with the stated goals, it is better to part ways early lest the issue fester into an all out infection within the ranks. History will repeatedly show that mutiny can follow dissention. No single individual is so important that they should be allowed to negatively impact the group as a whole. This goes back to general preparedness and skills. Should the individual(s) in question have certain skills necessary to the lifeblood of the group, it would be wise to find others with similar skills to mitigate the control these individuals enjoy. This is good planning anyway, because what would happen if this one critical person were to become ill incapacitated or worse? When we get into training and skill sets, we will present options to increase the resilience of the group to attrition and turnover.

Components Of A Good Mission Statement
There are a few components that make the framework of a good statement. They should be plausible, specific and inspiring. Without these concepts why would anyone believe in the mission in the first place? Let's examine the components of a good statement:

Purpose Statement – This defines the desired outcome, not the method of getting there.
"Our mission is to provide a safe and secure long-term survival environment for our friends and families after a severe disaster event".

How-to Statement – What activities will we do to accomplish our goals?
"By coming together with diverse skills and knowledge, we will provide for the necessities of survival through food and water production, shelter, security, health, safety and comfort of our members."

Values Statement - If you desire to include religion, or have any specific moral values you wish to make clear, here is the opportunity. Perhaps you wish to clarify your political direction or affiliation here as well.
- "We will make every effort to assist the hungry and not turn anyone away with an empty stomach."
- "We are a Christian group that will follow the teachings of the Bible."
- "We will adhere to the originally accepted United States Constitution and Bill of Rights and create no laws or rules in violation of these documents."

Additional Elements - There are times when you might want to add some information to explain your position, but keep it short and simple.

There is always room in other writings to define your goals in more depth. If you feel compelled, ask yourself the following questions as you devise your statement.

- What is the problem or need your group is trying to address?
- What makes your organization different?
- Who will benefit by this group?

Brevity Is The Key To Success

Try not to turn the statement into an essay. You should be able to use your statement as an elevator pitch when someone asks what the group is all about. Be sure to give others an opportunity to participate in the framework of the statement before it is finalized. You can write all you want but if others don't feel as if they have a say as to the group identity, they won't truly feel as if they are a part of it. Remember back when we discussed the *Independence Conflict,* most self-reliant people are by nature leaders to some extent and may quickly challenge any presumed authority.

Once you have a solid definition of who you are as a group, don't just file this document away to the dustbin of history. Share it, promote the concepts and beliefs that were identified *and build your group around them.* Show your sincerity by living by the values that have been identified. This is how you attract a following and harmony. Additionally, it will demonstrate sincerity in the mission.

Establishing An Oath

It's been said "there is no stronger bond between men than an oath." This is a good reason to consider an oath. Some will say that this sounds extreme, sounds too much like a cult, and not like a family group. Why would we want to go to the level of having an oath in our group? In actuality there are many very good reasons to establish an oath.

You thoughtfully worded a mission statement to remove any confusion of what the group is all about. Now that you have everyone on the same page and they've bought in to why they are here, ask them to pledge to support the group.

This does a couple of things, it has them verbalize that they understand what they are doing here and it gives them a sense of commitment.

The oath has been a part of organizations both fraternal and service for as long as people have unified for a cause. There is nothing "cultish" about verbalizing one's sincere commitment to others and the organization as a whole. When one raises a hand and repeats the oath or in some groups, an obligation, it becomes part of them, it binds them by conscience to their compatriots.

There is no guarantee that an oath will keep everyone in line and focused, but it should give him or her pause to be sure this is what they want to do and enhances the gravity of the situation. Anyone who laughs off such a pledge might be indicating that they are not sincere in their presence.

The oath need not be a long drawn out ordeal. Keep it well worded, sincere and realistic. The oath should reflect the mission statement to drive home the values and direction of the group. If a potential member refuses or shrugs off the notion of an oath, it could be a clue as to their ability to commit to someone other than himself or herself.

Tips for Writing an Oath

Here are some general guidelines, but it is the group's collective responsibility to finalize their specific oath.

Begin with something such as *"I (we) solemnly swear to...."* Then designate the purpose of the oath, for instance, *"I (we) solemnly swear to...equally contribute to the common survival and defense of the accepted members within* (insert group name).

Next, specifically add what a member will offer in return for equal acceptance in the group, such as *"I will commit my honor, my skills and my resources to the best of my abilities in accordance with the stated requirements set forth by the duly elected leadership"*.

Move on to ensure the understanding of the group rules, for example, *"I will abide by all laws, rules and regulations set forth in the founding documents. Furthermore, I will not violate the privacy, sovereignty or resources of another member, nor speak of any group activities, concerns or business whatsoever to any person or persons not authorized to be privy to such information. I understand the safety and security of our families and friends depends upon strict adherence to the rules. I accept these terms under my own free will and accord in the presence of..."*

The oath can be ended by witness of Almighty God, a named group leader, other members, committee, your Nation or other supreme entity.

Keep the oath long enough that when you say it out loud it has an air of commitment and importance, but no longer than about a page of text. The oath should be to the point and powerful. Be sure to consider any potential legal consequences because in some places an oath is a legal verbal contract. Take care to not add anything in violation of existing laws or the contract may come back to you with legal consequences

Law and Order

"In the absence of law and order, men revert to savagery"

Rawlesion Precepts

Now that you know *why* you are part of the group and where it's going, you are ready to face the problems of keeping order.

Without order the group is little more than a lawless refugee camp. The very nature of a survival situation will almost certainly demonstrate that people will do almost anything it takes to better their position or just endure until the next day. Just because you might have what many would say are people better prepared to succeed, doesn't mean your time together will be anything like a nice vacation away from the hustle and bustle of everyday society. In fact, this endeavor can be very challenging and extremely dangerous if undertaken without due diligence.

A note on current law. It is important to check with your particular state regarding the formation of groups. Some states frown on anything that resembles a militia or organized paramilitary group. It may be illegal to assign rank to any member of a group. This is a serious concern. Investigate this carefully to be sure you are not in violation.

Though the goal of most survival type groups is to be an asset to the community and not be seen as a dangerous force, your state or local legislature may define "militia" differently and it's important to do some background research prior to formation or structure.

The Dangers of a Lawless Society

"Things bad begun make strong themselves by ill."
Shakespeare

Unfortunately there are those that almost welcome the collapse of civilization, as they know it will bring a fresh start. They may feel as if they never quite fit in with daily life and structure. The romantic allure of joining a band of survivors and reforming society in their vision can be intoxicating.

Along with them will come the followers, those who are comfortable in taking part of this dystopian fantasy. They expect that their new life will be free of the bonds of a restrictive existence and they will be able to live out their days as if in a fiction novel where everything plays out according to the script.

This is human nature and for this reason it will be important to define the rules and what will be accepted of all members. The group should always be aware of its pulse. Always be on the lookout for animosity and resentment. Harmony is a difficult balance to achieve but it starts with awareness and communication. To understand trouble is to understand people.

As we continue you should begin to see the value of carefully vetting and then working closely with others. You are essentially bringing these people into your family. Every effort should be made to screen each candidate carefully over an extended period of time.

The Constitution

"The Constitution and the laws are supreme and the Union indissoluble"
                                                                    Andrew Jackson

The group is a living organism that must mold and adapt to change. Because it is made up of individuals with different philosophies and backgrounds, it is subject to internal stresses and external pressures. To control these forces the group will need structure. While it is true that fear breeds discipline, fear is not always the most efficient leadership style.

People for the most part seek structure, organization and vision. A look into the prison system will reveal how uncertainty and even subtle changes to everyday routine can have a detrimental effect on the inmate's moods and productivity.

Some people can only operate when they have a clear understanding of structure and most people appreciate routine, it gives them peace of mind to know what to expect.

A Constitution is a document that explains how the governing body will work. The document can provide for the separation of powers, which we as Americans can appreciate dearly. The United States Constitution provides the *super laws* that almost all other laws are measured by. Of course, there is a considerable leap from such a revered document and the constitution of a small band of survivors…or is there?

A look at the history of the United States, or the original colonies to be specific, will reveal that the roots of our Constitution served a relatively small citizenry.

Yet today it is the foundational document by which the greatest national power on Earth operates. So, don't underestimate the value of such a humble document. There are many such constitutions in the world today, ranging from small groups all the way through most declared nations.

Great care should be taken in preparing this document for the group. It has been noted by scholars that the most effective constitutions are *not* the most specific. When the *super laws* are too specific they become restrictive and cause friction in society. Nations that have attempted such clear control have a higher rate of State failure and many others are forced to scrap their constitutions and start again. Ecuador has had 20 versions, Thailand has had 17, the Dominican Republic has had 32 constitutions and the list goes on. A common theme among these failed documents was that they all had an excessive number of constitutional articles. Honduras had 375 articles and such high numbers are not uncommon.

The United States Constitution has 7 articles. The document has been amended 27 times and the first 10 amendments are known as the Bill of Rights.

There was a reason for the history lesson. Writing a constitution allows people to communicate across time with a consistent message. Operating from memory is subject to mistake and alteration. As with the other group founding documents, it is wise to carefully consider what goes into the constitution. Keep in mind that this document is intended to give powers, define limitations and allow for checks and balance of the leadership.

It is recommended that members become familiar with small government concepts and chain of command leadership structures to create the most advantageous system of governing.

The group may at some point in time be forced to scale up in size to form a larger community. All major cities began as the lowly village.

There is also the chance that your group will never be more than just a hobby group, a social club or it may even fail. The lesson here is to not take yourself too seriously or your members may get tired of dealing with you. Consider these possibilities when designing your infrastructure.

Those who choose to have a say in the matter are the ones who write the future. If you do nothing else in form of foundational documents at least establish a *Code of Conduct.* You will need something to anchor yourselves to when confusion reigns.

Rules and Consequences

Order is the key to a civil society. For the members to truly feel free they must feel as secure as possible. To maintain order it will be necessary to establish some rules.

Rules should be fair, just and apply to all members equally. For rules to be respected, a consequence will need to be applied for ignoring them. Punishments should fit the violation and be applied equally to keep balance. Always use the agreed governing structure to convert all proposed rules into official law. There is no need to re-invent the wheel when it comes to law and order. Most of us are aware of what is right and what is wrong.

When establishing the rule of law, take care to consider the ethical and moral consequences. Another oft-overlooked aspect when laws are rushed into service is unintended consequences.

Take the time to consider any adverse effects the new law may have. It is also wise to allow due process to happen in the case of a crime. This will strengthen the legitimacy of the governing structure in the eyes of the people.

Be careful to not enact too many rules or govern with too heavy a hand. For the most part, groups are peers and will require a horizontal leadership approach to motivation. If leaders apply a heavy-handed approach, resentment and non-compliance will begin to weaken authority on foundational levels. As the group grows you will find a cross section of personalities and values. It will be wise for leadership to be flexible to account for this. Too many regulations and too rigid a structure can cause interpersonal battles to consume precious time needed to achieve group goals.

Significant rules might include, but not be limited to:
- Life Safety
- Protection of personal belongings and resources
- Drug or alcohol abuse
- Common resource use: water, food, equipment, shelter, etc.
- Violation of membership agreement

- Structure of leadership, powers and limitations
- Currency and use of funds
- Trade restrictions and commerce issues
- Rules of Engagement (ROE) for conflict resolution
- Sanitation, infection containment
- Treason
- Mutiny
- Capital crimes
- Application for membership
- Separation or member removal processes

Safety First and Dealing with Attrition

Another set of rules to consider can be with respect to common safety, training and education. These will apply in some form throughout the life of the group. As the group expands and becomes more permanent, societal routines should begin to set in. As this happens, complacency and boredom may become a concern.

To encourage safety and prevent accidents with equipment it would be wise to develop safety protocols, such as the buddy system when working in dangerous environments or establishing ground guide personnel for moving vehicles. This will help to prevent accidents. It is also a good idea to assign the task of training and safety to a responsible person within a work group. Ongoing education will be important to keep a knowledge base of qualified people in the group.

At any time attrition (the loss of members) can have a devastating effect on key responsibilities. Attrition can deplete personnel through fragmentation, accidents, and infectious illness or even combat casualties. It is wise to plan several levels deep in every responsibility if at all possible. Rules for education may need to be enforced due to resistance to learn new tasks or operate outside of an individual's comfort zone.

Chapter 4

SOCIAL CONFLICT AND THE GROUP

"Fortunately, children do not need "perfect" parents. They do need mothers and fathers who will think on their feet and who will be thoughtful about what they have done. They do need parents who can be flexible, and who can use a variety of approaches to discipline."

James L. Hymes, Jr.

Privacy Management

This is a very difficult concern in the survival group. Any soldier can tell you what it's like to never be completely left alone and how old that becomes after a while. The very nature of the survival group runs in direct conflict with any sense of privacy. Some groups will have the benefit of living in their own homes and some will be forced into an existence more akin to sleeping in a shelter.

We will delve into the nuances of both arrangements later on but suffice it to say, make every attempt to give each other living space and respect their privacy. The saying that good fences make good neighbors has a proven value. The group should be prepared for personnel turnover due to a magnitude of reasons. As we have discussed, it is almost impossible to get any number of people to agree on everything.

If you find that there are members who don't wish to be there any longer, all you can do is attempt to find the root of the problem. This is where a neutral member such as a well-respected elder might be able to help.

Some people are just easy to talk to; they often don't even need to ask questions because everyone just openly confides in them. If you are fortunate enough to have such a person, draft them into service as the voice of reason. If we find ourselves in such a situation where the group is actively living together, people will need to talk and even vent frustrations.

It is important to remember that all organizations can only operate successfully by paying strict attention to the needs, aspirations and concerns of people. Successful organizations can trace their success directly to the amount of concern that they exhibit to the people they serve.

Even in a long-term survival situation, people will require a certain level of "customer service", for lack of better description. It may take some time to get to this point when there are many more pressing matters at hand, but it will become more important as time marches on.

Problem Members: The 3 Monthers

Part of the turnover problem may be a breed of folks that we'll call *the 3-monthers*. These are people that can keep up the façade of fitting in for about 3 months. You may notice that they seem to be a perfect fit, enthusiastic, helpful and always out front. Then they will begin to show little problems, conflicts, and attitude. Eventually, they will need to be removed.

These types seem to travel from place to place and always complain about everyone else. Something to keep in mind is that when anyone comes on too strong or works harder than others, they may burn out sooner.

Problem Members: HOA Syndrome

Another issue that occurs in the group environment is what we'll call *the HOA syndrome*, because there are similarities to a dysfunctional Homeowner's Association.

This is where a member in charge of something vetoes someone else's ideas because they didn't think of it first. Such disruptive behavior can be a serious problem and demonstrates personal insecurities.

Any person in a position of authority would be well served to adopt ideas and solutions of others if the solutions are in the best interest of the group.

Unfortunately, small minds will feel threatened and play politics out of spite or insecurity. If this continues, the group should take a vote of no confidence or apply a rule designed to remove the person from that position.

Unlike a peacetime organization, the survival group cannot afford to tolerate selfish interests that may endanger the morale, efficiency or survivability of group operations in uncertain times.

Problem Members: Cliques

In some cases the HOA syndrome will manifest by way of cliques. One of the fastest ways to tear down an organization is to allow cliques to continue unchecked. Leadership should be wary of these groupings and make every effort to dissolve them or at least mitigate any friction with others. Often, cliques are formed by some kind of common ground among the members be it ethnic, background, religious, regional or operational. Sometimes they are just friends that hang out together and fall prey to poor decision making due to a simple form of mob mentality. Cliques may be a symptom of a larger problem but are not uncommon. Sometimes people just have chemistry and prefer to stick together.

The problem members may be caused by stress, lack of discipline, and lack of respect or outright hostility toward someone else. The prudent leader will attempt to identify the problem, understand it, and control it through effective team management. Left unchecked, animosity can lead to trouble.

For example, a testosterone filled operational security team may resent non-tactical people as paper pushers or weed pullers to the point it causes hostility on all sides. These sorts of things will happen and only strong leadership will keep balance.

Synergy and Group Fragmentation

We touched on a couple of personality issues but there are some related concerns that the group should watch for. Regardless of what the personality conflict is, if left to smolder there will be trouble. Anyone who has worked in an office that has merged with another or experienced the prima donna employee will attest to the animosity that follows. Often these issues don't work themselves out and someone of authority will need to step in. A united community is important for the psychological health of the group.

Because synergy is a goal of the group, members will need to work through their problems. If left to fester there will be problems in every area of the group. Consider the member who feels slighted in some way. If this is not noticed and addressed, the member may begin to sabotage others as revenge. He or she may become a security risk by speaking outside of the group or worse, fall prey to outsiders and leak secrets in a desire for acceptance. Security within is always the first requirement to safety. If private information was to be made public everyone could be at risk.

Another concern could be fragmentation from within. Remember the clique situation? What if unhappy clique members begin to plot against other members? Rivals within the group will cause polarization, and this can spread from just within the particular clique to a full on split within the entire group. To extend the logic, this split could have ripple effects and end up with one side seizing everything.

There will always be an attempt to consolidate power by stronger personalities. Sometimes they feel it necessary to prevent others from having power because of dissimilar values or interests.

This is why it is so important to have clear group goals and values, and to have an attentive leadership structure to ferret out this type of disharmony before it gets too widespread and out of control.

But Why Is The Rum Gone?

During times of stress and despair people often turn to tobacco, alcohol and even drugs. In the survival environment, we can already anticipate that these items *will* be in short supply. For this reason it is imperative to secure alcohol and pharmaceuticals for medicinal uses and be watchful of thievery that could leave the group short on critical meds.

As the vices run out there may be psychological issues and antisocial behavior. We've all seen how a friend or family member's behavior can change drastically when these items are unavailable. In your rules there should be a way to deal with this. Keep in mind that these are family and friends and eventually they should be back to normal; so adjust the policy to the behaviors as needed. Once the behavior is back to normal, don't allow the stigma to continue undeserved or you may end up with the slighted individual we previously discussed.

Vices are not the only things that lead to withdrawals. An exceptionally large percentage of society is on medication with some form of behavior or mood altering pharmaceutical. In the best case, most people will only have a few weeks of medication. Once that is gone, there will be a glut of irritable people out there. There is a chance that someone in your group is taking some form of medication, whether it is for a behavioral condition or otherwise medical.

You can also bet that most people are not in a hurry to share the sensitive details of their conditions or medications. Expect surprises as people reach the end of their prescriptions. Some people may begin to worry and plead for a party to search for resupply. As time goes on and meds are not found, there may be serious anxiety to the point someone comes unglued.

Unfortunately there may not be too much the group can do other than to make efforts to stock up as much as possible in advance. Herbals may be an option but they may not be available either unless the group makes a dedicated effort to understand and produce their own through preparedness.

"Oftentimes when we're trying to turn our lives around, we concentrate on getting rid of what's not working: throwing out our junk, ending toxic relationships, quitting bad habits. But becoming the man you want to be can never be entirely about emptying yourself of the bad; you must also fill the newly created space with the good. We need people/hobbies/traditions in our lives that brighten the way and bring us joy and fulfillment."
                                                                Brett McKay

Depression and Group Efficacy

What happens to the human mind when we find ourselves firmly ensconced in an ongoing survival situation? What happens when days lose their boundaries and become little more than a once respected concept to measure time? We as a people are tethered to clock and calendar. If the clock becomes the enemy, and boredom settles in, so will conflict and poor morale.

Depression is the proverbial dinner guest of the idle mind. It never leaves. To combat depression it is important to keep the mind engaged in needful ways.

This goes for the group as well as the individual. As a matter of fact since the group is made up of multiple individuals one can see how important it is for everyone to realize that their behavior and effort is of vital importance to the group as a whole. It is often the smallest things that can bring comfort to distressing times. To help one improve his mental state, think about what is most important in survival and build backwards from there.

Survival is mostly mental. The will to survive is uncontested as the reason many people have made it back from impossible conditions. The will to survive is fueled by drive, drive is fueled by purpose, and purpose is a sense of having a job to do. If you have something to live for, you will move the proverbial mountain to do that job. So, one must realize his or her purpose. Notice I didn't say to ask yourself *if* you have a purpose, I said to realize *what* your purpose is. This is an important distinction. Your purpose may be to protect your spouse or children whereas a combat veteran may say his purpose was to be there for the guys on his left and right.

Never underestimate symbols. A symbol is something that you can use to focus your purpose. It can be something drawn or held in your hands. Remember the movie Castaway when Tom Hanks held onto the FedEx package and never opened it? He did that because he needed a reason to live. To him that package must be delivered. Your symbol can be anything; a lock of hair from a loved one for example can bring unimaginable strength to a person in need of inner strength. A religious item, a photo, even a picture of a place you would like to visit or retire to can hold immense power to a person.

Be sure to carry a symbol or personal or religious item on your body, not in a bag. Encourage everyone in the group to do the same.

Even if you lose everything else you own, that item will help you to not lose hope.

> *"If you're going through Hell, keep going"*
> Winston Churchill

Avoid Idleness

If there is too much time available to sit around it will seem as if time itself has stopped to most of us. Most people will fare better if they are being productive. Feeling as if one has a purpose can go a long way to keeping a person's metal acuity intact and ready for action.

An effective leader will understand that to prevent depression and conflict he must keep everyone engaged with productive duties. Be sure to avoid obvious busywork, as people will see through busywork if it is not thoughtfully designed and it will just annoy them. Now, getting someone to participate in chores or projects may be a whole other problem. Almost every group reports that apathy and differing priorities are a problem. The best way to handle such problems is to offer structure to the schedule. When people know what is coming and what is expected of them they are more likely to participate.

A duty roster that sets the schedule and identifies responsibilities is a useful tool. Try to avoid impulse tasks just because you are disorganized. With this being said it is also important to know when to work people and when to let them alone to their personal time. Be sure to provide time for social events and group meals.

Over time, people will adapt to their new group life and the group will become like family. There will always be some sort of problem and some people will leave but if the world is in a bad way, people will usually choose what they know as opposed to what they don't know and stay in with the group.

Tend to the Morale of the People

Another way to chase away the signs of depression is to keep the group members entertained. While it may sound silly to think about playing games or music when there are lives at risk, here is what Ernest Shackelton, famed explorer, said regarding the banjo and sing-a-longs with his men during the year and a half trek home from their doomed Antarctic expedition after his ship HMS *Endurance* was crushed by ice floes " *[they were] a vital factor in chasing away symptoms of depression."* Everyone benefits from a laugh. Once the situation allows, make time to decompress. Throw a football, play stickball, have contests to see who is fastest at a task to inspire competition. Even if it is to see who can set up a weapon system the quickest, things like this offer the added benefit of reinforcing skills as well. In time you may want to put on a play or skit just as a diversion to the drab work, work lifestyle.

If you want people to retain information and develop critical thinking skills, you must get them off task regularly so their minds have a chance to relax.

No matter how hard you try though, some people may not be able to adapt to the newest version of normal. If their behavior cannot be brought in line with what the group can tolerate they may have to leave. If all efforts have been expended the group will need to consider ejecting them.

Punishment and Ejection

Recently, a high-level group member relayed a story to me about old friends and a well-established group. It had to do with weapon safety. As they were shooting for target practice, one of the members had a weapon malfunction. In order to clear the jammed round he was struggling to unlock the slide on his firearm. The problem began when he was inadvertently pointing the muzzle at the friend next to him while struggling with the jammed round. When the operator was told about the unsafe conditions, the operator of the jammed weapon stood his ground and said he was not doing anything wrong.

There are two problems here. First, there is the unsafe handling of a weapon. Second, there's an attitude that he was not wrong in directing the muzzle of a weapon towards other people, especially while trying to clear a malfunction. To make matters worse, this was not the first time the member had been warned of muzzle sweeping his weapon. In this case a long time friend and member was immediately ejected from the group.

What conditions led to the poor handling of a weapon and what conditions led to the defense of such an act by the operator? On the surface I would say that a culture of safety had not been seriously promoted in the group and if it was, why had this member not accepted it? Secondly, was it pride or agitation that led to the member behaving in such a way as to disregard basic safety requirements and the stern correction of such unsafe behavior?

In either case something led up this incident. Both conditions can be prevented by not allowing complacency and apathy to fester in the group.

Make it a policy to stand up when it's important and let your members know that there is never a time to be unsafe.

Some people prefer to avoid conflict because they are afraid to offend someone at the initial signs of poor behavior. As a warning to your group, if you prefer to overlook problems, they may come back to haunt you. At some point nothing will help to remedy a bad situation or chronic poor behavior and removal from the group becomes the obvious choice.

Another example of a situation where rules must be enforced would be if a member has stolen from others.

There is little room in a survival group for those who have only their own interests in mind. It would be a good idea to develop a process to address crimes and violations.

Not every poor choice requires a hangin' but to maintain order and safety of other members something must be done. Here is an example of the process to correct and eventually eject a member for a small infraction that continues to be a problem.

1. Verbal warning to offender or family leader
2. Family is asked to correct the situation
3. Offender possibly detained if the problem warrants
4. Offender and possibly family is ejected from group.

If an infraction is outright disruptive or dangerous, ejection can be immediate. In peacetime the ejected member may be asked to leave and not return. What will you do in a world with no law? Most groups seem to draw the line based on the seriousness of the crime.

If it was a capital crime, then capital punishment seems to be the consensus. If the crime was not tolerable but not deserving of capital punishment, then ejection it is.

In some cases a member may get in trouble with the law during peacetime. The group will need to decide if the problem is serious enough to affect his membership in the group. For example, a member gets a DUI charge for driving while intoxicated. Is this enough to eject someone? What if the DUI was part of an ongoing alcoholism problem? Does that change your opinion?

"He that is taken and put into prisoner chains is not conquered, though overcome; for he is still an enemy."

Thomas Hobbes

Removal Procedures

In the event that members must be removed from the group, difficult decisions will have to be made. First, the group must define the type of offense where a member should be considered for removal versus another form of punishment. Assuming there is no enforcement of law, as we currently know it, it will be necessary to be reasonable and just in the application of punishment. Too often people foresee the notion of a world without law. Having only books and movies as references, some will lust for blood and petition for death for almost anything that may bring harm to the groups' survival. Previously we discussed how fear breeds discipline. This is true to a certain extent but eventually the people will shed the chains of fear, choosing to risk death on their feet than life on their knees. Conversely, if criminal acts are overlooked the group will eventually fail.

There is no easy way to make rules that will keep everyone happy all the time but the rules that are made must be just and carried out with equality and fairness to all members.

Of course there is the risk that the expelled member, knowing all of your secrets, may return with others to threaten your survival. A question that must be entertained is, is this risk worth a death penalty out of fear? Should a guilty member be incarcerated for a small crime? You can't just overlook some acts and over react to others. If the ejection has occurred in a dangerous grid down situation where there is no law you may want to consider what kind of threat he will pose with insider knowledge of your current situation before you turn him out.

If a member is ejected or otherwise decides to leave, that person should be entitled to the items he or she brought into the relationship.

This further reinforces the need for all members to have basic skills and supplies when they join the group. As we observed previously, the loss of a member should not be a knockout blow to the group.

Ejection and the Local Community

If a member has been ejected from the group it may be wise to contact any friendly groups in the area to give them a heads up. This would be more important if the crime was serious. If the member was just not a good fit for your group but may do well elsewhere, you may choose to let him go quietly.

NOTES:

Chapter 5

PICKING A LOCATION FOR YOUR GROUP

"A house is not a home unless it contains food and fire for the mind as well as the body."

Benjamin Franklin

Much has been written about where to set up camp for the survival group. We are going to break into two basic types of group for the location discussion. The *Survival Group* and the *Retreat Group*. Before we discuss physical characteristics of land we must consider the legal and financial arrangements that are most common. This way the survivor will know ahead of time the possible future ramifications of his or her decisions.

The Survival Group

The *Survival Group*, for this discussion, will be best described as a group that has a base location, and has developed a community arrangement allowing for all families involved to work and run the "farm" as a collective. This group can be setup in either a rural or an urban environment, though the rural is much more common. In the rural scenario, the property is usually a working farm. An urban group would most likely be more of a post apocalyptic group that establishes their "farm" in an abandoned area of a city to take advantage of existing structures for protection. Some groups choose, or have little choice, to set up shop in suburban environments. The suburbs can work better than an urban area for producing food but just as in an urban area, security will be a challenge.

Whether rural, suburban, or urban, the property should be large enough for multiple homesteads and all of the collective tasks required to support the members. Proximity to future resources is a benefit that should be considered if possible.

In a pre-event scenario, members may buy in and/or receive a piece of land or section of a property to establish their camp or build a living structure. We will call the people moving onto someone else's land or those who buy into adjoining land, *homesteaders*. In some cases a landowner will grant authorizations for others to share the land in exchange for active participation in the group.

There are some serious legal concerns that will need to be considered for both the primary landowners and the homesteaders. A primary landowner who invites others to reside on his or her land in peacetime may or may not charge for the homesteader's residency. In a time when all laws are still in effect there are rental provisions and rights available to the renters. One must consider these rights and be aware of the legal eviction process should a relationship sour. If the primary landowner outright sells a parcel of adjoining land to the homesteader and the relationship sours, he or she could end up with feudal neighbors in the future.

In addition, homesteaders who make the decision to take advantage of an offer to buy into, or depend on, an informal invitation to reside on someone else's land might be left out in the cold should the landowner change his or her mind in the future. Careful consideration should be made to be very sure that this is where you want to be.

It is wise to spend as much time as possible with others in the group, especially a landowner before committing finances and long term plans.

The Retreat Group

A *Retreat Group* is a number of people who arrange to meet at another location or rally point in case of activation. This location may be a home, cabin, or other location where the group feels all of their survival needs would be met. On a side note, a big box store, shopping mall or food warehouse is an extremely poor retreat location choice. If other refugees or panic shoppers don't get to you, law enforcement or military will. There will always be others better manned and better armed than you. As we will discuss in later chapters, when it comes to physical locations, an exit plan is critical, and these places are more like the Alamo than a retreat location.

Just like the full-on survival group, there are legal considerations as well as personal considerations when it comes to selecting the retreat location. This type of group usually has a property owner among them. The same legal and liability concerns apply. Rental of space, injury on your property, damage of property, eviction, etc. are all real world problems, especially while there are still laws in place. In a world without law, all bets are off and the survivor could find himself left out in the cold, or worse. Again it is prudent to be very sure that these are the people you want to be with in a crisis.

Characteristics of a Good Physical Location

A number of books have been written on how to select a retreat location. This will not be a comprehensive review of laws, taxes, gun rights, politics or demographics. We are not going to reveal any perfect algorithm used in selecting the best state to live in. This book is about forming and managing groups of people for the art of survival.

For the purpose of our discussion we will focus on the *characteristics* of good locations that will support multiple members. If you have the means and the luxury of selecting a piece of land on your own timetable, the following thoughts should help as a primer. If you are forced to select a place to camp or homestead on the fly, the following criteria should help remind you of the most important things to look for depending on your length of stay. These tips are also helpful when selecting a spot on someone else's land as part of a group. Think of it as choosing the best seat before someone else sits there. Just being aware of these criteria will better help you in your individual preparedness as well.

For a group that does not have the funding for a true retreat location you may want to look within. Ask if any of your members have some land, a sod farm, a warehouse or anywhere you can set up in the meantime. It is important to figure this out before you need it. The last thing you want to do is to take over a piece of property you do not own. At that point you become an occupying force and that will cause problems if the owners arrive.

An option is to plan ahead with a church. It has been said, *"it takes a village."* A survival village will benefit by having three basic components, a church, a security contingent and a way to produce food.

Many churches are situated on larger properties and are usually trusted in the community. This is a good option for groups that wish to support and protect their community as well. Not every scenario is Armageddon, and social good will help build group morale as well.

Finding the Farm for The Survival Group

The *Survival Group* is slightly different than other groups in that they are usually planned out well in advance and account for many families. Regardless of the legal aspects discussed earlier, the property must meet certain criteria to support life on a long-term (or short-term) basis depending on your situation. The short version of selecting such a site would be to look for a place that will provide for the 7 main areas of survival, yet be sustainable for the long term.

You are not likely to find a location that meets every item on the list, but at least you will know what to look for to help you choose wisely if you have the luxury. The list may be expanded as needed to suit your requirements.

The 7 basic areas of survival *as related to property* are:

1. *Security*
2. *Food Production*
3. *Water Resources*
4. *Shelter Resources*
5. *Health and Safety*
6. *Energy Resources*
7. *Communication.*

Location Security

Without a strong security plan, you really don't own anything you have. There are a couple of ways to look at this concept. There is the threat that people may try to take what is yours and there is the risk that Mother Nature may attempt to destroy what's yours. An easy way to get a feel for the land is to see it from above. Attempt to acquire a topographical map or aerial photo of the area in question. Actually, you should strive to have overhead Intel of all areas you operate in if possible. Maps will give you a better perspective of what is nearby, where the travel lanes are, and relationships to assets and liabilities.

To reduce your vulnerability to people and nature, look for some of the following characteristics:

Accessibility
o   Look for available roads, trails, water features, and landing zones.
o   Are there multiple avenues of approach and escape?
o   Will the area freeze, snowdrift or flood?
o   Will any natural event affect where you sleep, farm or work?

Defendability
o   Look at your area from an outsider's point of view. Where would you enter?
o   Can these areas be defended and in the alternative, provide protection in retreat?
o   Are you on the higher ground or lower ground?
o   Are there large open areas?
o   Are the avenues of approach defendable?

Concealment

- Will the current foliage provide concealment from observation? How will the change in seasons affect this?
- Can foliage be thinned out for sight lanes, or added to for defense purposes?
- Are noises, lights, smells and smoke from your camp likely to draw attention?

Transient traffic

- Is the area susceptible to people passing through?
- Are you near a travel way or in the shortcut between two places?
- Is this a popular area? Will others have the same idea?
- Are you on someone else's land? If yes, have you worked out all legal arrangements?
- What are the chances someone else may hunt here?
- Are there any other camps or settlements nearby?
- What is the threat level in this area? Have you done a hazard analysis?

Food Production

Whether you are there for the long haul or just a layover, food is still going to be a requirement. In some cases you may have supplies with you but it is wise to be aware of what nature may be able to provide. For the longer term you'll want to start producing your own food. This can be done in a number of ways. This is not a book about nutrition, but two things that you need to survive are **carbohydrates** *and* **proteins**. **Fiber** should also be added for digestive health. Make efforts to explore the bioavailability of nutrients in certain foods to stave off malnourishment. Choose those foods that will offer the best bang for your survival buck. Depending on the climate and resources available, the survivor can produce food through traditional gardening, aquaponics and various types of livestock among other methods.

Be careful to not overestimate your opportunities for wild edibles and hunting, especially with groups. History is rife with stories of hardened pioneers and Native Americans that have starved on the trail, perished from famine or malnourished into disease. Additionally, it is wise to plan for food preservation.

Consider the following when selecting a place to produce foods:

Food Procurement
- Are there edible/medicinal plants nearby?
- What is the wildlife situation?
- Are there opportunities for scavenging?

Food Production
- How much land can you dedicate to growing your own crops/raising your own animals?

- Is the soil conducive to growing? What is the soil composition: rocky, sandy, silty?
- What is the growing season? Is it short? Does the ground freeze?
- Is there room to expand the garden in the future?
- Is there a water supply for irrigation?
- Could flooding damage the fields?
- Can you keep livestock here?
- Could excessive shading by terrain or timber block the sunlight needed for growing?
- Is altitude a problem?
- Has there been any chemical or radioactive contamination in the area?

Water Resources

Water is the most important resource you will need in large quantities. Without water, you won't survive for more than a few days. In some climates you will become impaired and possibly incapacitated in just hours. Water is heavy and takes up space in storage, so you'll need to plan ahead. Everything you do will have to keep both of those issues in mind.

Water Issues

- Is there water near the location?
- Are all water sources able to be made potable?
- Is the water source from the surface or hidden by well?
- Can others contaminate the water?
- How will you transport the water? Is there potential danger or is it impractical?
- Is flooding a concern?
- Will the water freeze with the change of seasons, thus changing the practicality of using the source?

Shelter Resources

Exposure to the elements can be hazardous depending on the climate. Whether short or long term, it will be important to make a shelter that will provide for warmth as well as protection from heat. In the short term any number of structures can be pulled together, but for the long term you'll need something more substantial. Analyze your area for building materials in the form of timber, tunnels, caves or vegetation. It is important to remember that nylon camping tents are not durable enough to be used as long-term shelters. They will begin to break down after several weeks of constant use and will not survive direct sunlight or inclement weather for very long.

Shelter Issues

- Is there an existing shelter on site?
- What is the quality and sturdiness of the structure?
- If there is no existing shelter, is sufficient timber, construction material and firewood available for the term you plan to stay?
- Are there alternate building materials easy accessible?
- Is the land flat enough to construct shelters?

Health and Safety

When we talk about health and safety in this sense we mean, what dangers may be present in the area?

Hazards

- Are there dangers to the site from overhead such as damaged trees or uphill stones?
- Is flash flooding a danger?
- Landslide?
- Wildfires?
- Avalanche?
- Indigenous insects, animals?

- Weather events?
- Contamination?
- People threats?

Energy Resources

Energy is not only about electricity. In fact for the most part electricity is probably the easiest resource to adapt to living without. When evaluating a location to settle into, consider some of the following:

Energy Options

- Firewood
- Moving water
- Sun
- Wind
- Fuels

Communication

For the purposes of this chapter, communication means access to other areas for transport and information. Being able to communicate is more than just talking. Communication includes commerce, news, messaging and transport of goods and material. When considering a location think of whether you will be able to move about and associate with others. While it may be tempting to park the group in total hiding, there may come a time when mobility and sharing of information will work to your benefit.

If you are extremely isolated it may be very difficult to respond to threats in time or assist a neighboring homestead in case of emergency. That road goes both ways.

Communication by movement and radio

- Can you freely move in and out of your location
- Are there roads, trails or waterways?

- Are you aware of all settlements operating near you?
- Could you move between them if needed?
- Is there a network in place to share news and Intel?
- Is there a system of commerce in your area for barter of supplies?
- What modes of transportation do you have and will they work in this terrain for all seasons?
- Is there high ground to set up antennas for radio communication
- Are there other radio operators nearby?
- How will terrain affect your radios?

Again, you will not find the perfect location for every scenario. These questions are to get you to think before you commit to settling in permanently. If you are in transit and need a place to rest, many of the above criteria will still be relevant.

One additional aspect of the physical location that is very important is that in an emergency, the group must be able to escape.

Always have an exit plan and preferably have at least two avenues of escape from every occupied position.

Chapter 6

ROLES AND RESPONSIBILITIES WITHIN THE GROUP

"You cannot escape the responsibility of tomorrow by evading it today."

Abraham Lincoln

There are two different types of tasks in everything we do. There are *individual tasks* and there are *collective tasks*. Just as the names indicate, these are things we do on our own and things we do as a team. Within a collective task there are usually multiple individual tasks that combine to make something happen. For example, one person may perform the duties of a rifleman in a patrol, but the entire patrol moves as one to complete a mission. In a collective task, each person is completely dependent on another person to complete the mission.

The survival group will be faced with many challenges both in initial development and during activation. During peacetime, a combat arms military unit must operate with a dual mission where it trains for battle and also manages garrison life. When they are activated, their mission pivots to focus on supporting combat operations. The same thing must happen in a survival group. Theoretically the group may be activated at any moment should a significant event occur. By laying the foundations of organization, tasking and training, the group will achieve a higher level of success.

Analyzing Group Skills and Resources To Set Priorities

You will not have a perfect world. In fact you will probably have little choice of who is available and the skills they show up with. In this chapter we are going to identify many of the skills that would be supportive of the survival mission. You as the group will need to decide how to fill those slots as time goes on. Tasking requirements in the beginning before disaster with only a few people is considerably different than if you evolved into a full time colony in a world without law. It is important to identify your priorities and only advance into new projects when the manpower, resources and conditions permit. We would all enjoy a large scale aquaponics system, fortified perimeter, livestock and well tooled farm but that may not be immediately possible.

Begin by taking account of what you already have. Start with both your existing operations and personnel. What priority survival systems are already in place? Are they running smoothly and at a reasonable capacity? Perhaps it would be better to bolster those systems/projects than to start something new right now. Where do you stand on people? How many total souls do you have? What are their skills, strengths, weaknesses and burdens? How might you pair your members up with work?

Once your current situation is under control, only then can you begin to think about adding more work. You may find in your initial assessment that there are active projects that are not a priority right now and they may be delaying more important projects. If this is the case, put them on hold for now and reallocate the resources to something else.

It may be necessary to utilize highly skilled people to work in a capacity they want nothing to do with and know little about. This is where all that foundational work will pay off because they should appreciate the goals of the group and help.

After you are comfortable in the current situation, start the expansion process. You should identify a list of desired projects and assign them a priority. Remember to plan the work and work the plan. Plan your work and expansion so that members see immediate improvements in a way that gives them pride and momentum. If an opportunity presents itself where the group can benefit, then take advantage of it when you can. In a world where resources and opportunities are few and far between it would be foolish to pass one up.

The Importance of *Clearly* Defining Roles and Responsibilities

Of all the things we must consider when working as a team there is one item with exceptional, critical importance. This topic is so important that it can literally be a matter of life and death.

*The leader **must** make sure that everyone involved is completely clear of his or her roles and responsibilities related to the task at hand!*

I cannot emphasize enough how important this is! How many times in your daily life have you run into conflict because 1. you were reprimanded, or 2. you reprimanded another because something was not done or not done in a specific way? This is not uncommon and may not always be a life or death situation, but there can be consequences that affect everyone in the group.

For example, if you were finally able to get your teenager to do laundry, but they didn't separate the light and dark colored clothes before throwing everything in the machine, you might end up with damaged clothes and angry family members. Not a capital offense but still a waste of money.

On the other hand...if a gate guard didn't know that he was to count every member of a patrol coming back in from the field, and an extra person walked into the perimeter and began shooting, a simple lack of communication has now become deadly. This has happened more often than we care to think about.

When assigning a task use reflective listening and get feedback after you explain the task to make sure everyone is crystal clear on what they are about to do and what the intended final result should be. If the objective includes a sequence of tasks, finish up the directions with a plain language description of what it is that you are trying to accomplish. In the military this concept is the last part of an Operations Order called "The Commander's Intent". All this does is describe what we are trying to accomplish in plain simple English. Take a few minutes to ask each member what his or her role is to make him or her vocalize it. You will get a pretty good impression if they were paying attention and understand what is expected of them.

3 things that happen when roles are unclear:

1. **Gaps**. If no one was specifically assigned to a certain task, there will be a gap in performance. Whether or not anyone notices the gap, no one will step forward to do anything about it because *"it was not his or her job"*. This will lead to blaming each other because someone should have just done it or at least said something.

The leader may also be criticized for not properly assigning the task. This can happen when the person assigning the task is a poor leader, or makes assumptions that everyone just "knows" what to do.

2. **Overlapping responsibilities**. If multiple people think they are responsible for completing the same task, there may be a duplication of efforts, which wastes time and resources. Also, one person may do the task differently than the other, which will cause hostility when he or she feels the other performed the task incorrectly. Another problem comes when a member feels undermined, or as if they are considered incompetent. A simple assignment of responsibility has now become a personnel conflict, and as we talked about previously, could lead to tension, unhappiness and a break in-group dynamics.

3. **Frustration among group members**. There are two versions of issue. In the first example, a task wasn't properly assigned so a member jumps in to take responsibility and gets in trouble because they should have not done it because they were needed in another area. Or, everyone knew a task needed to be done but no one was doing anything about it. In either case, someone is angry because someone has trespassed on the responsibility of another, or there's been a complete lack of initiative among the responsible members.

Roles and responsibility is a two way street between leaders and subordinates.

An effective leader will strive to completely understand what needs to be done and what is needed to get it done. We are again circling back around to the basics of human relationships. Communicate with your people, gather information, ask for feedback in areas you are not clear of, and clearly identify what you want someone to do.

Never, ever assume that someone can read your mind or *should have known* something. Don't worry if the team is coming together at a snails pace, teams take a long time to develop and form deep, trusting bonds. These things do not happen automatically, they take time and practice.

With a clear understanding of how to properly assign tasks we need to figure out what to do first. No matter the situation you find yourself in, there will always be jobs that must take priority over everything else. In the matter of survival, the daily chores may be very removed from what we are used to. This will take plenty of patience and understanding from all involved. At the earliest possible opportunity, take a few minutes to let everyone gather their thoughts and understand what has happened and how the event has changed everything.

The Normalcy Bias

Most of us go about our daily lives in a relative fashion, we have bills to pay, jobs to perform, children to raise, etc. Within that realm of responsibility we are usually quite aware of what to expect within those areas of our lives.

Because of this awareness we can usually expect some small hiccups, like an overcharge on our cell phone bill or a bad grade on a child's test, and we've learned to deal with them as they come along.

It is even likely that we even entertain thoughts on how any of these areas could go horribly wrong, like a major car breakdown or a job less. As the survivalist/prepper you have most likely given more thought to this than most people. This is why you are reading this book.

With all of this careful thought and preparation there is still an area of human nature that may hamstring us in times of danger. Unless you have trained for crisis through active efforts, accepting the reality that you are experiencing a life-changing event may not be obvious. We see examples all the time. People hear gunshots and shouts but stand there trying to see what happened or take pictures instead of taking cover. When something so unusual or out of our ordinary occurs, we often freeze up or dismiss it as not really happening. This is sometimes called "The Normalcy Bias."

This same behavior may happen within a group at the beginning of a real activation. Each member should be prepared to deal with other's seemingly unhelpful behavior. It may not be that the helpless person is being malicious or useless; it may be that he or she is in some level of shock or acceptance of the new reality. Remember that these people may have seen terrible things; lost loved ones or have never experienced a real tragedy in person. This is especially true with younger people or children.

In order to move forward you may need to take a moment to accept the past. It may fall on someone in the group to take responsibility, gather everyone and openly acknowledge what has happened and that we are here because we knew this could happen.

Remind everyone that there is much work to be done and everyone is important to the effort.

You will find that all the organizational efforts you made before the event will pay off greatly now to reduce indecision and lack of direction. If it takes too long while someone tries to figure out what to do next frustration will grow, conflict and distrust in leadership will take over. The last thing we need right now is dysfunction.

After the event has been acknowledged, keep the minds busy with productive duties. When people feel a sense of purpose, they will be more helpful and healthier. Lets get started.

Situational Reports and Analysis

Understanding that we are here for the primary reason of survival it should be concluded that everything we do supports that goal. Of the many tasks to be done on a daily basis, there will be some that are more important than others. Take a moment now before we go any further and consider your group status and current situation. Every group will be different in its location, personnel status, health of members, seasonal climate, resource availability, and proximity to the retreat and vulnerability to threat. This is a form of *SITREP* (Situational Report), used to describe/define the current situation of a given person/group.

For example, if I asked you for a SITREP right now you might say, " I am in the bunker eating a freeze dried ice cream sandwich and reading a great book on survival groups. I haven't heard any gunfire in the last ten minutes." In all seriousness, the SITREP is used to communicate what your situation is to someone who may not be there with you to see it with his or her own eyes.

The SITREP can be used at any time but in this case it is a measure of unit status.

You may want to use the following list to see where your group stands in each area. This list is not exhaustive; feel free to include other topics that may affect your group. There are many tasks under each heading but some are more important than others. The list may look familiar but with the added category of transportation. This is due to the number of people involved and transportation may be a survival concern for the infirm.

You may desire to add something but most likely it will already fall under one of these main categories:

- Food
- Water
- Shelter
- Health and Safety
- Security
- Energy
- Communication
- Transportation

After completing your SITREP, first check to see if your group needs help in any critical areas, such as food or water. Critical areas should be addressed first when it comes to prioritizing work.

Interdependency and Combining Tasks

Since this is not a survival guide, we won't go too deep on *how* to perform certain survival tasks. What we will do is identify *which* tasks need to be considered for survival. Along the way you will begin to see some opportunities for interdependency.

This is to say that some jobs will naturally dovetail with others.

For example, most tactical and security work utilize similar personnel and equipment. Farming can combine animal husbandry and gardening. Cooking and food preservation utilize similar methods. It will be to the group's benefit to combine relatable tasks, assets and personnel into departments. This goes back to understanding the strengths and weaknesses of your members. Build on those strengths by putting the right people in the right job. Some families will have multiple skills. If this is the case, it may be wise to have them work in different departments. If for no other reason, at least it will help to reduce the impact to a department if a family leaves the group. It also helps to prevent a chokehold or monopoly in an important area.

Setting Priorities for Group Tasks

We are going to progress as if this is a new group in a new location. If you have an existing arrangement use this information to evaluate your status and possibly refocus your efforts. By doing this you will be strengthening your group by ferreting out gaps and blind spots in your operations. In a later chapter we will discuss *blind spot analysis* and *gap analysis* in more detail. We are wise to be reminded that a survival group may only get one chance to activate for a disaster. It has to work the first time and for the duration. This means attention to detail and organization wherever possible.

So what are the priorities if you were to arrive on scene for the first time? You can always follow the *Rule of 3's* as a quick reminder of what's most important in survival. When linked to the main areas of preparedness we discussed earlier, you begin to see where the priorities lay.

Look at these rules of thumb and think of how they relate to your situation.

The Rule of 3's:

- 3 minutes without air

- 3 hours without shelter in severe climates

- 3 days without water

- 3 weeks without food

Security is Priority Number One

Now, if there is one important adjustment to the Rule of 3's, it's that SECURITY IS ALWAYS JOB ONE! In a world of uncertainty where the biggest problems usually come from people it is important that the group feel secure. Without security, you cannot safely perform any of the other functions. When people do not feel secure they will have a lower morale, they won't be inclined to go outside to perform the chores needed to sustain the group. Eventually there will be an erosion of confidence that things will be ok. This may be more of an issue in a threat environment but it needs to be at the forefront of all activities. The reason for this is simple, a threat may materialize at any time. For a threat to be most effective it should be planned with an element of surprise. Don't let the bad guys surprise you! To mitigate the intended surprise you should be prepared through a series of active and passive actions.

Again you should start to see a theme that runs through this book:

Planning + Awareness + Skilled action = Success.

Security is an ongoing process. Security is provided in layers through community observation, intelligence gathering (sometimes referred to as "Intel"), aggressive actions (such as patrolling for area denial), Observation Posts/Listening Posts (OP/LP) and in some cases active kinetic actions against others by way of spoiler attacks or quick reaction force (QRF) response to threats.

It should be expected that the vast majority of group members would not be well adapted to full time survival operations. Most people in society today are accustomed to a better condition of living than generations past and are barely able to take their eyes off their cell phones for 30 seconds a day, or lift more than a couple of grocery bags from the family SUV to the kitchen. It would be counterproductive to demand or even expect that every member will be a natural homesteader and SEAL Team 6 member in their spare time. This would be especially true in the immediate aftermath of major disaster or event.

The best way to build confidence in your members is to demonstrate quality leadership and understanding of their hardship. It will be important that every member have a role to perform. If a member is asked to perform a duty, make sure they understand their role. Clear well-defined roles will reduce friction and uncertainty.

Security can be a difficult task to manage in a hostile environment, especially if the group is comprised of members who are not able or inclined to fight. One of the scariest scenarios would be kidnapped or attacked family members while they are working outside.

It is important to provide security at the perimeter of all operations to prevent these occurrences.

It is also wise to use armed patrols in a high-risk environment to reduce the opportunities of threats to observe your camp. And, bear in mind that while people are the most common problem, wildlife may also rank highly on the list of threats to members. Have you done an analysis to discover if there are threats from bears, wolves, mountain lions or other predators?

Group Resources and Support

It is also important to make every effort to provide members with as much material and support as possible. No one likes to feel like they have been turned out to the trenches without the tools they need. With this being said, we know that in a true survival situation. There may not be proper equipment. This is why priorities must be considered. If the task to be done is lacking in resources, is the task all that important? If it is, you may need to designate support from the tinkerer in the group to come up with a field expedient solution.

Types of Daily Activities

We briefly touched on this but there will be concurrent activities on most days. There are usually four types of activities going on at any given time for the established survival group.

o Daily Chores
o Special Projects or Operations
o Training Operations
o Security Operations

Daily Chores

In the daily routine members will be working together to provide for the common welfare of the group through chores such as:

- Hygiene
- Child Care
- Education
- Sanitation
- Water Collection
- Food Production
- Food Preparation
- Food Preservation
- Firewood Collection
- Livestock/Animal Care
- Laundry cleaning and repair
- Hunting/Trapping/Foraging
- Scavenging or obtaining resources
- Equipment and shelter maintenance

Special Projects or Operations

Items in this category will be those irregular operations that may require that manpower be diverted from other areas. For instance, this may be a multiday trip for hunting or scouting. It could be a spoiler attack on another group that is threatening. It could also be something like building a new structure, digging a new latrine, canning after a harvest, or preparing a seasonal crop. When thinking ahead for climate changes or seasonal chores, try to keep these kinds of projects in mind so as to not come up short.

Training

Somewhere in the schedule you will need to make the time for training. Since most members will not be competent in all skills, it will be imperative that a training program be initiated as soon as possible. This will greatly contribute to the overall preparedness of the group. Most members will probably be competent in some areas of survival but you will probably be lacking in several areas when it comes to expertise.

It is for this reason you must know what skills are available and what is lacking. It would be wise to sit down with the committee members or whoever is assisting with the leadership to identify any shortcomings.

The next step is to make a plan to fortify those skills by pairing unskilled people with skill holders or holding workshops to create a broader knowledge base. If this is not done and members are lost for some reason, there may be no one to perform critical tasks.

There is another less obvious benefit to training, staying busy. They say a busy mind is a happy mind. In times of stress or danger an unoccupied mind may wander to dark places, having severe effects on wellbeing and morale. A strong leader will find a way to keep everyone mentally engaged to offset this. Many people enjoy working toward achievable goals.

Give them a reason to stay engaged. A more recognizable benefit is safety. There is an old military saying, *Never let the ghost of a young soldier say, "If only I was properly trained."* Take the time to develop your people.

If you have the luxury of a retreat location where you can stockpile supplies, consider building a library. The library can be digital, there is nothing wrong with that. We may as well take advantage of the ability to store massive amounts of data for reference later. But, never count on anything that requires power. Back up your library with physical books that are relative to survival.

I hear a great reference idea to have is a book on **Survival Groups**.... Wonder where we could find one of those? Shouldn't be hard to find, only one book on the topic has ever been written and you are holding it!

When selecting books, think of all the skills that may be needed in a long-term event. You can use the categories of survival we discussed earlier as a guide. It would be wise to choose reference books on skills you don't have or may be complicated, such as medical practices, foraging or gardening.

Another set of helpful books would be reference materials on raising animals because even if you don't have animals now, you may later. It would be good to know how to care for them, diagnose illness and breed them. With that possibility, pick up a few books on goats, rabbits, horses, chickens, etc. You never know what may come and which skills you weren't able to acquire before the world turned upside down. While we are all waiting for that to happen, take this opportunity to secure all the reference materials possible.

There is no way to know or remember everything, especially in a stressful situation. Some groups form a training library and share books among each other. A good meeting topic would be to get some sort of accountability of what books the group already has and which subjects to add to. You may even start a book club as a form of training and then do a group project based on what was learned. We'll talk about how that works shortly.

Be sure to also choose some age appropriate books for the little ones too. Books will be a valuable commodity when skills are lacking and for the purpose of relaxation and enlightenment during dark times.

Security Operations

Remember that Job #1- every single day, every single night, is security for yourself, and for the group. You'll have ongoing daily chores and activities but you must also provide for the task of security. We know that security never takes a day off. 24 hours a day 7 days a week, the security plan must be performed with discipline and proficiency. This can take a toll on personnel. We are not going to dive into specifics of the duty roster but every able bodied person in the camp must embrace the dual role of their daily duties and perform security in some capacity, even if it is just in reserve.

We touched on security earlier and how a layered plan is best. The size, skill, health and armament of your group will dictate the level of protection you can deploy. Too often, people over estimate their abilities and underestimate their situation. It may not be wise to try and conquer a thousand acre farm with four men and a few dependent family members.

Choose your battles and take every advantage available to you. If you are a small force, make use of terrain, early warning devices, Intel gathering, etc. The best case for the small group may actually be invisibility. Sometimes you may be able to hide in plain sight and sometimes you may need to disappear completely.

When you reduce your target size, you have the opportunity to reduce your security commitment. It would be wise to study small group tactics and defense then train for proficiency.

Training includes drills, collective tasks and individual tasks. Marksmanship is also very important and should be practiced as often as possible.

Marksmanship was a major factor in winning the Revolutionary War as small bands of colonists successfully defended themselves against the world's most power military at the time.

Active and Passive Defense

There are concepts called *Active Defense* and *Passive Defense*. The group should analyze their situation and decide which method will serve them best. Because each group will be different, there are different options available to them. If you are small, you may want to not attract attention. If you are well organized and strong, you may not be too concerned about attention or would prefer to project power. These are tactical decisions that should be made as early as possible.

Passive Defense means being less than obvious and giving the impression that you're less prepared than you really are. It does not project the impression of power. There may be no outward signs that there is any security in place. If there is security in place it is well concealed in an attempt to prevent detection. Other passive measures might be fences; tactical landscaping and other measures that assist in the fundamental measures of **deter, delay and defend.**

Many of these measures don't necessarily scream out to the enemy "I have guns pointed at you." A passive defense may also be used as a deterrent to attack. This is where the enemy is aware that you have forces to react but you are not aggressively postured. Remember, if you look like a great location that's worth protecting with roving guards and a large wall, you might attract a lot of unwanted attention.

If your retreat looks like nothing special, maybe the marauders will move on to the next location.

Active Defense is more obvious. There may be walking guards, observation towers or other aggressive measures in plain sight. The idea here is to project power, to say, "We are armed so keep moving." While it may sound like the way to go, you'll want to be sure you can back up what you are saying here. Even Mike Tyson had to fight in prison. There is always someone who likes to challenge authority, especially if it looks like you have something worth fighting for. Such a posture also screams, "We have food and medical supplies."

Whichever method you choose keep in mind that situational awareness, readiness and action are the keys to security. One thing that may be a concern in a group is the differing backgrounds most people will come from. When building a security team, you may have people from different branches of military or law enforcement all trying to work together. Usually when you get tactical types all on one team they revert back to their training and that training will probably be different among them. It will be important to find common ground if they are ever to perform as a team. A proven way to accomplish this by creating a *team charter*.

The Team Charter

"We can succeed only by concert. It is not "Can any of us imagine better?" but "can we all do better?"
Abraham Lincoln

Teams are a great way to accomplish complex tasks, but if they are all moving in different directions friction will reign. It is imperative that a team work as one, especially when the chips are down.

There is no room for independent action when everyone else expects you to act as a team.

What is worse is if you thought you were doing the right thing at the right time and confused everyone else. The training we discussed earlier can reduce this confusion. But what if there are fundamental differences in someone's understanding of a particular member's role on the team?

This is where a *Team Charter* can help. The team charter is a document that defines what the purpose of the team is, how it is organized and what is expected from them. It is best to establish the charter as soon as the team is defined but it can be created later for a team that is struggling. The charter sets the stage of understanding and expectations immediately, thereby reducing any "history" that might get in the way of working together.

This is not a complicated document but the time spent on it up front can save a lot of headaches and trouble later. Of course, it is understood that some of these techniques may be impractical if your group is on the run and just surviving until tomorrow is the goal. You will truly see the benefits of these proven processes in the longer-term survival scenario with a set location. Just attempt to get organized as soon as possible, it will pay off in big ways.

The team charter may vary depending on the team's mission and makeup but that doesn't mean it needs to be changed all the time, quite the opposite actually. Keep it simple and consistent. A security team will have a different charter than a construction team or a medical group. All of the mentioned groups may be made up of members who come from very different backgrounds but have a similar knowledge.

The charter will help the team achieve specific goals together. This is why it is so important to get them on the same plane of understanding.

Begin by addressing three components:

o   What is the reason for the team?
o   What is the team expected to accomplish as a whole?
o   Why is the team's mission so important to the group and how does it fit into the overall mission?

Setting Up the Team Mission

This is more important when the team is doing a project. If the mission is tactical in nature there is a whole different set of planning orders called operation orders, but that is for our next book (Stay tuned). The charter is better used when the combat team is first organized. In some cases a verbal meeting may suffice.

If there is a danger of personal agendas or confusion of the standards to be used, clear that up before the team sets to work. This may be the most important aspect of organizing a team. A survivor group will be much different than a commercial venture but many of the efficiencies concepts remain relevant.

With this in mind, organize a project or mission with measureable and time bound goals to keep things on track. There is not a lot of time for drag and error in the survival environment. In locations with extreme weather or seasonal climate changes, you may have a small window of time to complete tasking.

Establishing the Team Makeup and Personnel Roles

Identify who is on the team and how they can best be matched to the various jobs within the mission. Because of diversity among the members, be sure to identify any special language, communication issues or required standards as soon as possible.

Remember earlier that we covered the makeup of a group. Try to not violate the effective *span of control* by keeping teams to about 7 members for good communication. Be on the lookout for any gaps between skills, resources and desired mission goals. Surprises are bad when the job is important. Be sure to identify who is in charge and what everyone else's roles are. Be clear, this is important. Identify who is responsible for certain outcomes and explain the outcome desired in clear terms to that person. Use good communication skills such as reflective listening to verify that instructions are understood.

Identifying Conflict Between Members and Roles Within The Team

In most cases, you'll be able to spot conflict rather quickly, but some people don't understand how to balance multiple tasks and communicate problems to leadership. Unfortunately, many people today are not well versed in live person-to-person conversational skills. The digital age has created a generation of personal isolation. Because of this, pay special attention when delegating assignments, or assessing skills so you don't push people into a potential conflict situation.

Setting Limits

If there are limitations on what the team is allowed to do or use, make that very clear in the very beginning.

Note that this is important with all members of the group. People do not always see the bigger picture. You may be surprised at how industrious and resourceful some people are. The last thing the group needs is for a team to cannibalize something or "re-appropriate" a resource that was needed somewhere else. If the team is tactical, the limitations may fall under the *Rules of Engagement.* Make the ROE clear and useable in the field to prevent rogue movements or unintentional conflict with neighboring groups or communities.

Team Specific Use of Resources

If there are limited resources available, make sure the members understand what they have to work with. If a team is tasked with a mission or project, be sure to give them the tools they need to accomplish their goals to the extent possible. Morale and effort will crash quickly if the team is hung out to dry without the requisite support. If you cannot support the mission then maybe the priority of the mission should be reevaluated. If the mission is deemed critical then strong leadership will be needed to motivate the members to persevere in the face of adversity.

Assessing Team Feedback Pre- Mission

This is where the team and the group leadership meet to ensure that everyone is on board and understands their roles. It is also used as feedback from the team to verify that the mission is achievable.

Lastly, *all team members need to sign off on the charter.* The gesture is more symbolic than administrative. The sign off indicates that everyone is committed to the team goals and agrees on everything above.

The goal of the charter process is to unite the team by establishing who they are, what they are here to do, what the team's responsibilities are, what rules they are to follow, who's in charge and what they have to work with. If your team is small and informal at least communicate the above information through conversation.

The Directory of Specialized Skills

Many opinions are available on what makes a group work but it all boils down to the quality of members, their level of preparedness and the skills they bring to the table. We know from experience that there is a very slim chance that any group will have the perfect formula for success. This book is designed for use at any level of group reference from the individual without a group all the way through the well established survival organization. As such we are dedicated to making every effort to be as complete as possible in offering information.

The following is a list of ideal skills the group should strive to acquire for a strong community. It should be noted that many of these are not a priority and may not apply to your situation at all. If every member of your group has at least the basics of survival, and the will and attitude to rise to the challenges of the survival situation, you are well ahead of the masses. As you grow there will be opportunities to learn new skills and possibly add new members to the roster.

So what kind of specialized skills would serve a group in the aftermath of a long-term event?

Medically Trained Personnel

Preferably begin with a field medic who is used to operating under austere conditions and add physicians and nurses whenever possible. You can never have too many medics, especially when first aid supplies and facilities may be in short supply. The group medic covers much more than basic first aid, as the medic should be monitoring the groups overall health, both physical and psychological. They should also monitor group safety, overall and welfare and any sanitation issues.

Poor sanitation practices have the potential to bring great illness to the group by way of disease. The medics should also conduct regular training to all members whenever possible to increase the general medical knowledge of all group members. This will aid in times of mass casualties or illness. Also consider adding veterinarians to the group, especially if you plan to have livestock or pack animals.

Mechanics and Mechanically Inclined Personnel

There will always be a problem with something that requires a repair or MacGyver type of solution. Never underestimate the person whose mind understands how things work. The tinkerer will save the bacon many times over. Sometimes they aren't social butterflies but leave them to their work and you will see great things.

A good mechanic has the skills needed to get things rolling and engines working. This will be handy when dropping the old car off for a repair is not an option any longer. Keep in mind that dealership mechanics have relied on computers quite heavily. You may need the hobbyist or the older guy who can tell what's wrong with an engine by listening to it, not plugging it into a computer.

Food Production / Farming / Livestock

There are many ways to produce food. Under this category you would consider all of the non-traditional methods of farming and gardening, including but not limited to aquaculture, permaculture, foraging, sprouting, etc. Also include such skills as rabbit production, general livestock skills butchering or other skills that produce or create nutritional foods.

Child and Elderly Care

Most groups will have children or perhaps elderly members that will need care daily. The reason for dedicating a role to this is so that parents can free up time to work on other things throughout the day. When children are old enough to hold responsibility, they should participate in group duties when not learning skills or taking part in education sessions.

Educational Staff

Teachers bring a unique benefit to a group. In addition to teaching, they usually have skills and experience in dealing with difficult people. They may be useful if there's a need for a voice of reason or mediator between group members. Teachers also know how to approach training from an organized perspective. They can layout a lesson plan that should adapt to any topic if you provide them the information.

Blue Collar Skills

The reason for such a broad title here is because there are so many job descriptions that could be included here. This goes back to the basics of the group and its SITREP. Ask yourself what skills are desired and keep your eyes open for the right candidates.

This group can include the strong backs needed to keep the firewood coming in, and the imaginative tinkerer able to streamline processes used to complete chores, and other miscellaneous jobs.

Cooks and Food Preparation Staff

Everyone will need to eat. Don't underestimate the power of a decent meal. Your situation will dictate the menu but a good cook can make an old shoe taste good. Cooks usually understand nutrition and can work to balance diets and any special nutritional requirements.

The cook can also coordinate with the food producers for quality and suggestions of menu items. In some cases families will be responsible for their own meals, in this case a cook may be able to help educate those who struggle in the food prep areas. Cooks also have a good knowledge of meat cooking temperatures and sanitation, two big health concerns that have the potential to very quickly bring illness to the group.

Vegetarians will have trouble without supplements of B vitamins and Iron in the diet. A good chef may be able to come up with ways to mitigate this issue.

Hunters and Trappers

We always make it clear that hunting for food may not support the survival group. When you have multiple mouths to feed the math has a tendency to work against you. Every skilled survivor should have a basic understanding of nutritional needs in the homesteading and labor-intensive environment.

It is sometimes misunderstood how much protein is needed to maintain and even grow muscle mass. You will need meat to stay strong.

During a serious event, the woods may become full of others who wish to hunt the same areas. This will cause problems and possibly collapse the wildlife system in the area, as you will have an influx of individuals and potential conflict between skilled and unskilled hunters. With this being said, skilled hunters are a great benefit to the group.

They will also see tracks and evidence of trespassers in the area. Trappers are also a good thing to have around as they can set many traps and snares simultaneously, this enables them to hunt in many places at the same time and doesn't usually require firing a weapon thus potentially giving away a location. It would be wise to have trappers and hunters teach others their skills. This will allow more hunting parties in the future and puts fewer burdens on them.

Scavengers

These are the people that you hand a shopping list to and somehow they bring things home, a special breed of people with initiative and the thrill of the hunt. They usually work with the tinkerers and understand the multiple uses of things.

These types will probably need to be told where to *not* go because nothing is off limits when they are on the hunt. This would be important should they choose to take the wrong stuff, like supplies from military units or militia groups. If they get caught it could end badly for everyone else. Army Scouts are exceptionally good at this, as are some teenagers.

Seamstresses

If the survival situation lasts more than a few months, clothing will begin to fall apart. This is especially true in damp or swampy environments. Sewing skills will keep the troops clothed and teach those that missed out on home-ec class how to handle a needle and thread.

Military and Security Personnel

As we said previously, security is always the first duty. Military veterans have the benefit of understanding how to operate in bad conditions, sometimes with no support and even less equipment. Some vets will have almost of all the skills we already mentioned.

However, it's also important to mention that not all veterans or military personnel have had the same training. Just because someone claims to be a veteran doesn't mean they are guaranteed to be the next Jason Bourne. In fact, a large portion of military veterans worked in jobs very similar to civilian "paper pusher" type positions, ensuring very little tactical or security training. This is where the background check and interview process for a new member is especially important.

I always support putting vets first based on my own military history and in my experience, they will get the job done. However, one of the problems that can arise when you mix civilian and military minds is friction.

What you absolutely do not want is a vet who does not play well with others because that will only be trouble later. Don't be in a hurry to move a bullet chucker to the front of the line, check him out for stability first.

Civilians usually don't understand how vets think and may have trouble working with them due to the determined way they operate. Mix this fact in with weak leadership and animosity can develop, especially if you have a high-speed combat team. These guys can save your bacon or take your bacon, so choose wisely.

Ham Radio/Communications Personnel

Hams are often electronics people. They can be invaluable to communications. Often they are tinkerers and can explain how to set up field expedient antennas and radio rigs. Unfortunately it is harder to find a Ham that has much in the way of homesteading skills than one would think.

There is much more to communications than just the amateur radio aspect. Commo is all about moving messages and hearing what is going on somewhere else. You may be lucky enough to find someone who has a good working knowledge of what makes a radio reach out further and how to speak with brevity, use encryption, establish codes and even non radio methods of communication such as message drops, geocaching, etc.

Primitive Survivalist or Homesteaders

This category is added because these are the skills that a group will definitely use on a daily basis. Again, you may not have a large group of people and those that are with you may not be proficient in these areas. These people will help you in the most basic of areas of survivability in the woods and as you conduct homesteading operations. It is also wise to build a reference library of books from generations past to gain lost insights to live in tough times.

Toolmakers/Engineers/Blacksmiths

There will be a need for tools and since it is unlikely the hardware store is an option, you may need to make your own tools. Engineers do have a use in the aftermath, even if there are no computers or CAD programs for them to use. One thing to consider is that engineers, like some military types, tend to have a rigid way of thinking. It's hard to achieve perfection in bad conditions and that could throw them for a loop. They will be more useful down the line when making calculations and building things.

Gunsmiths/Experts in Ammo Reloads

The gunsmith will be able to repair and improve firearms. This may be valuable when people are carrying them around everyday. The Reloader may have a spot in the group if there are tools and supplies to support his work. If ammo is scarce the Reloader can be a valuable asset.

Self Defense

At some point any member may find themselves responsible for their own survival. If they have access to basic self-defense skills it will help them with that responsibility and also build confidence, teamwork and physical conditioning. If you find someone who can teach others some good defensive skills, it will have a big impact on group morale.

Solar/Alternate Energy Experts

Energy, for the most part, is not too difficult to survive without. However, there are many advantages to having power. Forgetting all the digital conveniences, power would be needed for charging radio batteries, lighting or electrical tools. Power tools will save tremendous time and labor when building projects or shelter, and lights will make medical work a lot easier to conduct than lanterns or candles. Creating electricity requires more than just good intentions. Along with mechanical skills to build the power generating equipment, the group could use someone with electrical knowledge in the fields of solar, wind and battery power.

Be sure to look out for alternative skills such as small engine conversion, gasifier construction, bio-fuels and even hydropower. There are options for human power generation and that may be a start but it is very labor intensive. The equipment that actually creates or captures the power is not very easy to construct from raw materials. But it can be done. It would be a good idea early on in the group to determine the methods by which the group will generate electricity and make a plan to collect the materials, which can be expensive.

Bee keeping

From sweeteners to antibiotics, honey is a genuine multi-tool of the survival world. If you plan on growing your own food, bees will be necessary for pollination and placed in the right location the hives might even become a pretty decent part of the security deterrent. If you find someone with apiary knowledge and experience, they may be of significant value to the group.

There may be more skills not listed here or some of these may not be needed within your group. Since there is no way to know what your group's status will be at any given time, you may want to just keep these suggestions in mind for the future. During peacetime it seems easy to remember it all and think you have a great plan. During a real crisis, rational thought and organization has a tendency to fall to the wayside. Choose your direction and priorities wisely, then attempt to strengthen your team with people who have the skills to build a solid community.

Remember to not compromise your values or lower your standards just to attract someone with a desired skill or it might come back to be a problem later. Skills are only a part of what makes a good survivor. He or she must also demonstrate a compatible personality, health, attitude and commitment to the team.

Don't forget the people that come with the candidate. Family members can be a serious concern to the group's morale and resources. Even if the main candidate is everything a group could want, the accompanying family members could be freeloaders, mental cases, and destructive or even thieves.

You are building a team and that team has a goal of winning every day. Remember, losing in the game of survival is not an option.

Group Finances

Operating a group can require significant resources if the plan is to function as a community. The plan should be that every member arrives with the predetermined amount of survival supplies but it may be a stretch to ask for a member to provide a big piece of equipment. Such systems could include, power generation, bulk medical supplies, rack storage systems, farm equipment, radios, library, farming supplies, rent, mortgage, repairs, insurance or other operating costs. Some groups choose to form legal arrangements to conduct their finances and some actually become operating businesses.

Options for fundraising could come from selling surplus supplies such as honey, foods, woodworking, farm tours or services. Another money maker could be to offer classes in homesteading. This may be a good choice to help prepare people in the nearby communities thus reducing potential refugees that may come banging on your gate in times of trouble. An added benefit would be the interaction with the community and potential for an informal intelligence network.

The choice to operate openly should be made carefully. There is nothing wrong with a business farm but you may want to keep the survival motives private for security reasons. On a side note, you may want to keep any non-traditional security out of sight. Some people are very perceptive of such measures and it could potentially draw unwanted attention to the group

Chapter 7

TRAINING, TEAM BUILDING AND GROUP PROJECTS

"Many people trying to do quickly what they do not ordinarily do, in an environment with which they are not familiar."

Dr. Kathleen J. Tierney
Disaster Research Center, University of Delaware

Just because a group of people finds themselves together in a situation doesn't mean they are capable of performing as one, no matter how motivated they are. Training and regular teamwork projects are necessary to develop the cohesiveness needed to better their chances of success. This chapter is not about the specifics of training but should be used as a catalyst for thinking about how to foster individual teams and the group as a whole. We are going to discuss reasons, proven tactics and methodology to get the new team to work as one. This information is not limited to starter groups. The advanced group should find useful information within to sharpen the edge of their teams.

Why should we use group exercises? When a team is first organized, regardless of whether the members are strangers or familiar with each other, there will be a couple of different initial responses. First, a group of strangers will most likely not initially speak out or participate for fear of sounding silly or they may wish to observe the other personalities to get a better feel for whom they are working with.

The shy approach may just happen because there may be a strong personality that can't help but to speak out in what he or she sees as a vacuum of leadership.

Secondly, if the group members are all familiar with each other, they may bring personal history to the group that gets in the way of progress. Either way, the mission will suffer if there is friction or the members are uncomfortable in speaking out or asking questions. Well-organized group exercises will force everyone to participate as a team and break down the walls of animosity and self-confidence. The group will enjoy more open communication. The exercises will facilitate sharing of information and expectations among members.

By improving the social bonding through team exercises the group will reduce that awkwardness of being around relative strangers. Members will relate and understand each other better, which in turn will increase loyalty and trust. These exercises will also show who is not a team player and may not be compatible with the group's stated goals, which is a very important piece of information to know early on.

Getting the Kids Involved

Additionally, it is a good idea to extend age appropriate training to the younger members of the group. These will be your replacements. Start training and teaching them as soon as possible. The more they know and are capable of, the less babysitting they will need and they will be better suited to become productive members of the group. If the training is fun they will embrace it and learn quicker. Make sure to observe extra safety precautions and abide by all laws as to what they can participate in.

Kids will bring plenty of energy to a group and that energy needs to be expended in order to settle them down. Kids today seem to be lacking in critical thinking skills.

If you can devise training that requires the kids to think outside the box, you will be doing them a great service. Such thinking will develop resourceful young adults.

The best way to learn or reinforce a skill is to teach it to others. Have the kids teach each other skills whenever possible. This will go a long way to developing tomorrow's leaders. Any of the scouting types of skills are a good start. Be sure to supervise them appropriately, especially around the younger members for safety. Sometimes kids forget or ignore safe practices. This is very important around fire, water, weapons, knives and animals. Strictly enforce accountability for actions as well as accountability for their locations. If someone is missing, stop everything immediately. Regular headcounts can help in this area.

Family Activities

The survival group is about so much more than tactical training. While security operations are a very important piece of the survival puzzle, that kind of training doesn't appeal to everyone.

There are countless activities that can be scheduled. If your training schedule is sparse it is not because you've already learned everything, it is because someone hasn't planned something to do. The best way to prep your family is to participate in training *as a family*.

Keys to a strong group include solid relationships and a catalogue of diverse skills being offered regularly that will appeal to all ages and skill levels. For inspiration take a poll at the next meeting by asking what the group would like to do in upcoming classes and events. As a primer pick up a book and make a list of a few skills that match the group's stated priorities and have some suggestions ready to go.

Classes in homesteading, survival or tactical areas can be held almost anywhere and be made fun. Fun and interesting are key points to consider when planning group-training exercises. Participating as a family will also help strengthen individual family bonds, making the entire family better candidates for a survival group.

Teaching Others

"First learn the meaning of what you say, and then speak."

Epictetus

When offering a class or training opportunity be sure to be prepared and have everything ready when people show up. Most people have very busy lives and will be turned off if you are disorganized, late, boring or not knowledgeable in the subject you are teaching. Most of all make safety your priority at everything you do. For many of these people this will be the first time they have done such things.

If you don't know the topic inside and out, don't teach it. That is a big problem in our business today. Just because you read it on the Internet or went to a free meeting in the park doesn't make you qualified to teach it yet. Do *not* misinform others. Build a class, verify the facts, steps and safety, be proficient at the task yourself, and only then share the information. If you aren't sure of something, do not make it up.

Getting Started With Exercises

Here are some tactics for improving participation, communication and trust among members. This is essential to get a team off on the right foot or refocus a group that has found itself in a rut. Don't underestimate the benefit of team building methods.

If nothing else the fun that ensues will bring people closer together.

Team Building Exercises

There are three simple types of exercise you can introduce to a group to speed up the teamwork:
- Getting acquainted
- Normalizing
- Ice-breaking

When people first meet they have the tendency to communicate through small talk. This is good but it doesn't achieve much in the way of effective communication. They usually don't ask real questions of each other and will guard their personal opinions and private life. This is to be expected given the reason the group exists. Privacy and OPSEC should be respected until one becomes comfortable in the group.

Getting To Know Each Other Exercises

Just as it says, this is where members will gather together and essentially interview each other. There is no need to be extremely probing here. The goal is just to get to know each other better. You can pair up or have a group discussion, just as long as everyone participates.

- What do you want to know about each other?
- What do they think their strengths and weaknesses are as they relate to the group's overall mission? Family, physical, health, etc.
- How can you avoid bringing their weaknesses into play? This is a question that needs to be asked now, not after something happens. I.e. A health issue, PTSD, certain conversational topics, etc.
- What do they like and dislike about group work?
- Are they more independent or do they like the social bonding of teamwork?

- How do they see themselves contributing to the team or group?
- Do they have any skills, hobbies or life experiences that would be good to know about?

Again, the goal here is not to interrogate but to get acquainted. Don't pressure or intimidate. You want everyone to be open, honest and comfortable, you are building a team and a family. Getting people to open up will foster trust and form bonds worth fighting for.

Other ways to get acquainted and have some fun:

Playing card mixers – hand out playing cards and have members seek out others to complete a "hand". Best hand wins. This helps people to open up in a fun way and work together. It also draws the quiet ones into the conversation, as people want to see what cards they have.

Jigsaw puzzle match - each member is given a piece of a puzzle. Members find others with mating pieces. Along the way there is conversation. This helps people speak to others who they may not normally approach.

These are meant to be fun and there are other ideas that can achieve the same goals. Just because you may be planning to live in a bunker during the apocalypse doesn't mean everyone has to be stone faced serious with each other all the time.

Survival will have its moments of tragedy and hardship but there will be a lot of downtime until the balloon goes up. Building on camaraderie will pay off in big ways later.

Normalizing Exercises

Normalizing is a way to get people to know what to expect from each other and the group as a whole.

Hopefully you considered creating the *team charter* we discussed earlier. This is the most straightforward way to clear the air and start a team off on the right foot.

Ice Breaking Exercises

This is a team-building concept that will move beyond getting acquainted. These are fun tasks that the group will do together. The tasks will encourage interaction among members and will reveal how each other works. The experiences gained from doing these tasks will help members bond through lighthearted and enjoyable teamwork. If you want people to participate and take things serious, give them a chance to lighten up, improve morale, and have some fun.

Many times groups fail because they seem to meet over and over with the same results. Boring meeting, nothing accomplished, unreal expectations and unhappy members, doomsday never arrives. After a while you start to notice that membership wanes, people have more important things to do and the group stalls.

Consider having friendly team competitions. Organize group tasks of different areas of survival such as setting up a piece of group equipment or build a lunar survival list of equipment. Maybe have members list what would be needed in a specific type of threat such as pandemic, tornado, etc.

These fun exercises are meant to inspire critical thinking, which may be the most important survival skill there is. Do you have some time left during an evening meeting? Challenge groups to build towers from straws and masking tape. The tallest freestanding tower wins within the time limit.

These fun and games should be conducted soon after the group is formed or immediately after the get acquainted and team charter exercises for maximum benefit of ice breaking.

Working As a Team:
The Crawl Walk Run Approach

"Coming together is a beginning; keeping together is progress; working together is success."

Henry Ford

Ok, you've done your team building exercises, you've gotten to know each other and you're ready to begin working as a team. By now everyone should be familiar with each other and ready to get to the meat and potatoes of why we are here. This involves learning new skills, reinforcing old skills and having productive meetings.

As we all know, there is a lot to learn when it comes to survival, especially within a group. Focusing on actual learning, there is a process that will help everyone understand and become proficient without too many headaches. The best way to teach a new skill or process is using the *crawl, walk, run* approach.

Just as it sounds, the method defines the tempo to which the lesson or drill is performed. Imagine your team wants to learn a skill that has multiple sequences. Begin by clearly explaining the task and drawing diagrams if helpful. You can use a whiteboard or a sand table it doesn't matter. A sand table is a square of dirt where you create a diorama using anything laying around to represent structures, terrain and personnel. It's like making a dirt map.

When it is time to do a demonstration, begin at a *crawl*. This is literally in slow motion. If the task is tactical, take it to an open field so everyone sees each other's positions. Save the woods and darkness for later when the task is well understood. Once everyone understands their role and is ready to pick up the tempo, advance to the *walk* phase.

The walk phase is just a little quicker but not real-time speeds. When it looks like everyone is clear, move to the *run* phase. This incremental training method will expose any gaps or miscues so they can be addressed immediately.

A very important phase of all trainings, missions or meetings is called an *After Action Report (AAR)*. The AAR is important because this is where everyone gets the opportunity to critique what went well, what went wrong, and what could be improved. Everything is on the table.

If you want your team machine to work, you need to tune it, test it and maintain it. Be sure to revisit plans and training regularly to keep people interested and skills sharp. If something needs to be updated, make sure it is communicated at all levels.

Improving Group Dynamics

The teams are working, but could they work together more effectively? Have you seen one group working well together and another group seems dysfunctional? Is there a morale problem because of a member who criticizes everything, and other members are afraid to speak up at meetings because of this? Maybe there is a member who always interrupts with a joke or snide comment.

These behaviors will derail a meeting and cause others to lose interest. We have to face it, in our line of work there is going to stress and problem behaviors. There is no way around it. This isn't to say we need to ignore these things, but there are ways to reduce their impact and possibly even fix the behaviors. A negative team will just not operate at its peak ability but a positive team can move mountains.

What are some causes of poor group dynamics?

Weak leadership – when a team has a weak leader someone else will attempt to take charge. They always do. This can cause fighting among the members, or a loss of focus on the mission.

The Yes Man – this happens when certain members/leaders blindly agree with authority. The yes-man ignores the other members concerns; eventually the others will give up speaking their mind, participating in duties or worse. The yes-man will volunteer the team for anything and will lose the respect of the other members.

Disrupters – there may be people who block group communication flow by being aggressive, too outspoken, misleading or even silent. Often there will be someone who always criticizes other people's ideas. We touched on that in another chapter with the HOA syndrome issue. There are also some members who just never speak. They are in attendance but don't participate. You may see a person who always likes praise so they dominate a discussion or boasts about themselves. Then there is the comedian, interjecting a joke all the time and disrupting the conversation.
Sometimes members will not put too much effort in because they feel as if they are being judged too much by other members.
They feel that it is easier to just keep their head down and do just what is required and little more. Of course this behavior draws the criticism that the member was trying to avoid. Then there are the shammers and thieves. These are the people who are never around when it's time to work but show up for meals.
Unfortunately these people may be sneaking into the pantry when no one is looking and stealing food or other supplies.

We would hope to trust everyone but when there are family and hangers-on involved, that may not be possible.
Additional things to watch for as indicators of trouble within the group:

- Member friction
- Lack of participation / poor effort
- Disinterest in expressing opinion
- Gossip/drama
- Forming of cliques
- Bullying/abuse

Minimizing Disruptions and Resolving Conflict

In any group setting, conflict will arise it is human nature. A strong team will embrace this fact and use it to their problem solving advantage. A feeling of imbalance, personality conflict, trust issues or just stress usually causes problems. For example, there may be accusations of someone not pulling their weight or acting in a way that is not helpful. It may just be that the conditions we are in are uncomfortable, dangerous or there is a stagnant feeling that we should be doing something different.

It may just be opposing viewpoints. One thing to remember is that conflict is a component of highly functioning teams. This is because of strong personalities and diverse backgrounds. Diverse teams are usually much more effective at solving problems than those that come from similar experience.

The team members must remember this and not let their differences affect the overall job at hand. Unchecked, these differences can turn into full-blown disputes.

As a leader the best bet is to start by addressing the problems quickly.

The leader has the challenging job of keeping his team on the rails and moving forward whether there is too much to do or not enough to do. Some people will deal with conflict by ignoring the problem. Some will assign blame and some will attempt to correct it by negotiation or stern action. Whichever way you choose to deal with it, keep in mind the goals of the team and the overarching success of the group must take precedence. If you have a problem member, pull the member aside and let them know how they are affecting the team.

Find out if something is going on that's causing the behavior because it may be a symptom of another, larger problem. Next, be sure that everyone understands his or her role on the team. If the problem member is not the leader, let them know that the leader needs their support. If they are the leader, they need to start acting like one or maybe they don't belong in that position. For thievery, it may be necessary to secure supplies or restrict access to certain areas. Refer to your group rules on punishment or removal or problem members.

When a team crosses over into conflict territory, the leader has some options available to get things back on track. The process will require patience and respect. This will almost become a mediation process. The effective leader will strive to keep opinions constructively balanced and not allow negative attacks on each other.

There are three areas where conflict will affect us: emotions, perceptions and actions. We will need to address all three to resolve the conflict effectively.

o Prepare for a resolution
o Understand the situation
o Reach an agreement

To prepare for a resolution you must acknowledge the conflict exists. Sounds odd but sometimes we don't realize we are in a conflict. Is there a problem or is this the way the members normally communicate? Some people just operate at a level of aggravation and it works for them. Some people thrive on lively debate and just naturally speak louder than others. These are the kinds of personality traits

Next you need to let the team know how this is impacting the mission/project and get them to agree to cooperate to resolve the conflict. If a party is too strong-minded to allow this, the problem will continue.

To understand the situation let each side present his or her view. Give them a chance to speak their peace. This will go a long way. Allow the participants to clarify their position. List the facts assumptions and beliefs in each position.

Once everyone has had a chance to speak their peace either the problem may be more readily corrected or the leader will need to step in and make some command decisions to reach an agreement.

The best course of action is to try to keep conflict under control. This is not as easy as it sounds but regular communication, respect and self-discipline will go a long way. If conflict happens, deal with it sooner than later. Don't let it get personal and don't look to lay blame. Take ownership of a problem or mistake and don't let pride or ego get in the way of clearing things up. You will gain more respect if you show that you can admit wrong rather than grumble and try to pass blame.

All teams need to learn to work together this is why team building exercises are so important. Keep the teams active; don't let motivational rot settle in through inactivity. Sometimes it may be necessary to rotate members among teams to keep people fresh. This will in turn help with the cross training that is truly needed to keep the group skills diverse and strong.

Reducing Conflict When Adding New Team Members

Anytime someone new joins an existing group there will be some disconnect. There is a window of time when a new member to a team will probably not fit perfectly and will be hit with a learning curve. This is normal and should be expected. A new member should realize that first impressions are lasting.

The new member has the responsibility to put his or her best foot forward and attempt to learn how things work before trying to make an impact that may backfire.

The rest of the team is also making an impression and it would serve them well to also make a good impression. The leader should make introductions and see that the new member is made to feel as if he or she is among friends, and understands roles, rules and expectations. As soon as new members are settled in, it would be advised to start some team building tasks if possible. For the group on the run, this of course will take on a different meaning. Refer to the *new membership* chapter for strategies to properly welcome a new member to a team. The listed methods are useful when members switch teams as well as joining group initially. See the chapter on new membership for strategies to get new members off to a good start.

Chapter 8

PLANNING FOR CONTINGENCIES

"A written plan can be an illusion of preparedness if the other requirements are neglected."
Enrico Quarantelli

The survival group is an exercise in readiness, flexibility and sustainability. Though we may have certain scenarios in mind where the proverbial stuff hits the fan, we cannot guarantee what might actually happen. In order for your group to truly be prepared, it should adopt an all-hazards approach. This is not to say you shouldn't be ready for a total grid down apocalypse or financial crash, just take some time to consider some of the other possibilities that could, and regularly do, happen hundreds of times every year. We are not going to cite lists of statistics about flooding and other natural or man-made disasters here. Suffice it to say, the climate is having an increased presence in our lives by way of disaster.

The survival group should be flexible enough to respond to most contingencies. In order for the group to respond, the members will need to understand what constitutes activation. While a tornado can be absolutely devastating to those in its path, the path will be relatively narrow. If you live in tornado country, there should be a contingency plan to contact members and provide for their lodging and welfare following a storm that damages their home. The same should be considered for flooding, wildfire or any other instance where a member is adversely affected. Some groups will go so far as to have an extraction plan to retrieve families under hostile conditions.

Any such plans should be well documented, rehearsed for viability and updated regularly.

Completing a Hazard Analysis

To prepare your contingency plans you must look at your surroundings with a critical eye. Begin with your immediate location and work outwards as far as desired. This means, start where you sleep and consider the likely hazards first, then keep imagining events up to and including solar weather and systemic collapse if you so desire. This process is called performing a *Hazard Analysis*. There are several components to this process.

First, there are a few terms to know:

- A **Hazard** is something that has the *potential* to negatively impact you.
- Your **Vulnerability** is how *susceptible* you are to the hazard.
- Your **Risk** is the level of *probability* that the hazard will affect you. What are the chances it could happen?
- The **Impact Analysis** considers the probable outcome of the event as it relates to you. How could this hazard *impact* your life?

By identifying the potential hazards, your vulnerabilities and the risks of hazards in your area of operations, you will be well on the way to creating a solid situational understanding of your location.

As a starting point, ask yourself if any of the following hazards are possible in your area. Planning to relocate? What does the new area's location look like?

- Drought
- Flooding
- Wild Fires
- Terrorism
- Tornadoes
- Hurricanes
- Land Slides
- Dike Failure
- Martial Law
- Earthquake
- Cyber Attack
- Rail Accidents
- Winter Storms
- Chemical Spills
- Physical Attack
- Land/Rock slides
- Pandemic or Epidemic
- Explosions – Accidental or Intentional
- Chemical, Biological, Radiological or Nuclear Attacks (CBRN

Could any of the above hazards trigger additional problems? Could a wildfire damage the vegetation that holds the slope together cause a mudslide when heavy rains come? Could an earthquake damage a nuclear plant or water dam? Could snowfall collapse a roof? Might a pandemic cause the food distribution chain to grind to a halt and the power to fail? This could lead to nuclear plants being left unattended to become overheated. We all know what happens then. How close are you? Where are the prevailing winds?

There are other situations that will warrant a contingency plan but may not be labeled a hazard per se. It will be important to think outside the box here

How will you react for these contingencies?
- *Structure fires*
- *Tear gas attack*
- *Total Evacuation*
- *Ambush situations*
- *Requests for charity*

- *Emergency requests for membership*
- *Request for support by another entity*
- *Retrieval of a lost or kidnapped member*
- *Active Shooter in perimeter or structure*
- *Different types of assault on your position*

You may have additional hazards to consider, which is ok. Consider the *risks and vulnerabilities* of each hazard to help you decide where to focus your mitigation efforts and reaction plans. Think of how you may be vulnerable. If possible, try to mitigate or harden against the hazard. For example, if you are in hostile territory, security may trump earthquake preparedness on the list of things to worry about.

For those who want to truly be ready for anything, you'll want to look at cause and effect. By this we mean, connect the dots. Every action has the potential to initiate another action in domino fashion. Look at any of the above hazards and ask yourself the question: "If that happens, what other problem could it create for us?" There is an exercise that would make a good meeting topic called *The Hazard Tree*. This critical thinking exercise will help to get members involved in planning and mitigation efforts while at the same time identifying any *blind spots* in your planning.

The Hazard Tree Exercise

This is essentially a flowchart that begins with a hazard and reveals the way that hazard may affect your surroundings or situation. The hazard is the first domino; you imagine the rest of the dominoes from there.

As you can see from the example hazard tree, a thunderstorm can have serious consequences when you play it out.

The severe storm creates lightning, which starts a brush fire which in turn causes a power outage and structure fires. Travel routes can become gridlocked and ultimately there could be a loss of life as the dominoes fall. The hazard tree can be used on any catalyst hazard to reveal your vulnerabilities or other hazards. Sometimes a hazard can cause other hazards.

When sketching out a hazard, try to think it through by levels. You will begin to see something very interesting. The paths, or dominoes, begin to tie into each other and ultimately require similar responses from the survivors. This is a very important observation and here is why. Many people feel that they need to prepare for a myriad of scenarios. While there are many ways for a disaster event to affect us, there are truly only so many ways we can prepare. This leads to why most emergency agencies are moving to what is called and *All Hazards Approach.*

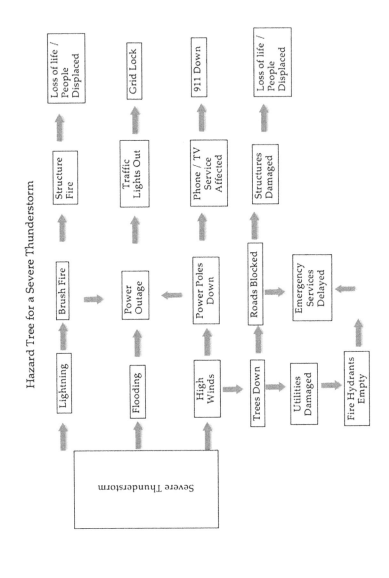
Hazard Tree for a Severe Thunderstorm

All Hazards Approach

This builds on what we just observed from our hazard tree. For our purposes we will adapt the approach to a non-agency type of group. What this means is, while we borrow the concept from front line emergency responders, we are not such an agency. The all hazards approach offers plenty of crossover concepts that will be very helpful in emergency management planning for the group.

The approach also has the benefits of calming the survivor's nerves. Much of our anxiety comes from feeling ill prepared. When you realize that your preps are useful to mitigate several similar areas of emergency, you will begin to feel more confident in your preparedness and able to proceed forward thoughtfully. Also, there are many benefits to your operations.

You will free up finances, reduce duplication of efforts and equipment, require less manpower and increase flexibility among personnel. This approach will also smooth your transition to a worse case scenario should things change during an event, and they often do.

An example of crossover training/planning might be in response to an unexpected fire. Would responding to a fire be much different than responding to a physical attack on the house? Except for the shooting part of course. In both scenarios you must deploy an emergency response. In both scenarios the house may still be on fire and/or casualties involved. In both cases you may need to evacuate under pressure and in a hurry.

The idea is to simplify and combine similar responses wherever possible. Most importantly, practice, rehearse and then add injects into the scenario after everyone has a grasp on the basics.

This kind of active training makes people feel like they are doing something useful, which keep them interested

What kind of overlap do you see in your plans and equipment? Be creative and think resourcefully about this

The Hybrid Tree Exercise

Below you will see a hybridized version of the hazard tree that we've developed. This tree injects student responses into the hazard situation dominoes to reveal decision outcome possibilities. It is one thing to identify hazards and subsequent effects; it is another to foresee how your decisions may affect the outcome of a situation. The reason we created this exercise was to force critical thinking. The tree will also reveal additional needed skills and equipment as well as identify gaps and blind spots in your plan. As you create a decision or identify a hazard, look at the entry with a critical eye. Don't just write it; think what skills or equipment may be needed to complete this action. For example, if you write "Apply CPR" consider whether every member knows the latest version of CPR. If you wrote "Extinguish Fire" do you even have a fire extinguisher?

The hybrid tree creates a visual graphic showing actions, equipment, skill deployments and how it all ties together. Remember the story *"For want of a nail, the war was lost"*? The hybrid tree is a tool that can help identify those *nails* and help you prevent a similar tragic outcome. There are countless ways to use this exercise, the challenge is to keep the meeting on track and not get wrapped around the axle in too much discussion. Identify any shortcomings and establish priorities to correct them. This one task alone can provide you with meeting agendas and interesting training opportunities for the foreseeable future.

MAGS: The People Part Of Prepping

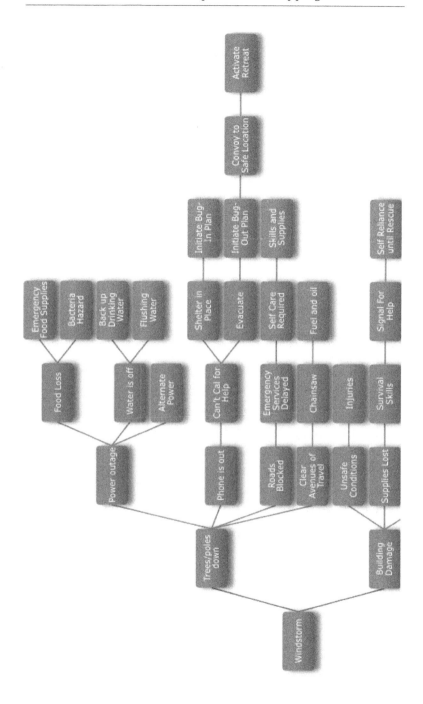

Trigger Points

Now that we have identified our immediate hazards, let's see what kind of outside influences could set a disaster event into motion. We won't delve too deeply into this subject because it falls outside of the scope of this book. The goal here is to help you better understand the bigger picture.

In our globalized society, events that happen great distances away can have direct or trickle down effects on anyone, anywhere. By paying attention to your news sources you will be alerted about geopolitical or natural events that might disrupt supply chains for everything from food to vehicle parts to the very fuels we need to mobilize. Throughout history there have been many global events that have affected even homegrown resources that our society needs.

During World Wars I and II, everything from metals to food and even labor from the home front was in short supply. In the aftermath of the great japan earthquake of 2011, a large portion of the Japanese manufacturing process was disrupted. This led to auto and other machine parts shortages globally including here in North America. If there is a serious engagement between north and South Korea, the electronics, auto and appliance industries will be seriously affected. When we say that you should be open minded about trigger points we mean to watch for *trends* that may not always be obvious or immediate, not necessarily specific events.

In some cases a trigger may be hidden within a smoldering issue, such as the unrest spreading through the Middle East or the euro financial situation. In some cases, a specific event could wreak havoc such as a bank holiday where everyone tries to withdraw their money at the same time and the banks close.

Pandemics, trucking stoppages, large-scale cyber attack or even an Iranian sea-mine deployment in the Straight of Hormuz could send world economies into a frenzy that tips the dominoes toward chaos.

Ultimately, there is little one can do but to be aware of trigger points and prepare for the potential trickle down effects on our daily lives. The key with triggers is to not go down the rabbit hole to find them. Just keep an eye open, think through your plans to be sure you have prepared as much as possible for any impacts and go on about your daily routine. Too often we observe people that try to make something from nothing, at least nothing concrete. They usually end up spreading rumors and becoming detached from the true task at hand, preparedness and survival.

Usually these notions come from hearsay, or some online forum warning or blaming of a *False Flag* attack. While there is such a thing as a False Flag, it doesn't directly affect your planning. A False Flag attack is a covert military operation used on one's own people or forces. It is designed to deceive in such a way to make people believe that an enemy caused the action. The use of false flags has been verified on numerous occasions throughout history as an excuse to gain public support for a "retaliatory" attack on the enemy. Due to the controversial nature of this tactic we won't get very specific with respect to examples in this book. Suffice it to say that the best orchestrated false flag attacks are very hard to prove.

At the end of the day it shouldn't distract you from your goal of being prepared for anything.

The more appropriate trigger is called a *Black Swan*. This is an event that causes other things to happen. Imagine the first domino in a line, when it falls the rest begin to topple. An event being labeled as a Black Swan is usually the result of hindsight when people try to figure out what started a series of events.

The only problem with a black swan is that the event is usually so subtle, few people even realize it occurred until several dominoes have already fallen. When a bad event happens, you should be more concerned with the current situation and actual survival, not the perceived motives behind the event.

How To Formulate A Plan

You've done all the research; you've identified your hazards and potential problems. At this point you should be exceptionally well informed as to your situation. Congratulations, you are arguably more informed than the greatest portion of the your population. So what do we do now? How do we convert that knowledge into something useful?

There is a concept that I learned the value of long ago when it came to leading people and it applies to most situations. *"Knowledge is usually not helpful without the ability to apply it."* If you are a statistical consultant maybe, but just because you are well read on the topics of field surgery doesn't make you a surgeon. It takes a little more than sleeping in a fancy "express" type of hotel to pull of a complicated maneuver. You need a plan and practice.

Lets start with a plan. There are several steps to formulating a plan. Done in the proper order and well considered, these steps will get you within throwing distance of your objective.

To increase the odds in your favor, you will need to refine the plan until it works and then maintain it just as you would with any other piece of equipment. So what are the steps? Below is the easiest format for creating a plan. **The beginner should start here**. Once you have the basics down, revisit the plans that require a higher priority and reinforce them.

An important principle to remember when developing emergency styled plans: base the plan on what people are *most likely to do* rather than *what they should do*. This is because during an emergency people often do what they think is right for them and may ignore directives by someone else. This refers more to those who do not train to follow a plan such as families caught in a fire or have nowhere else to go. When the plan is designed to achieve a specific set of goals and regularly practiced, you can be specific in what you want people to do.

Formulating The Basic Plan

Identify the problem – begin by using one of the natural hazards gleaned from your hazard analysis.

Form a team – who will be the players in this plan? What is the leadership and chain of command?

Understand the situation – what is the hazard and how does it affect you? What are the consequences should this occur?

Determine your goals and objectives – what do you want to happen? What is the <u>ultimate</u> objective? Your objective should be more than "making it like it never happened." The objective will describe the preferred outcome of the situation.

Identify courses of action – this is the meat of the plan. This is where you say how you will deal with each contingency with specific plans of action. Write down who will do what, what will they do, how will they do it, what will they use to get it done and when does it need to be done.

Identify contingencies – if it can go wrong, you may want to prepare for it.

Prepare the plan – this is where you bring it all together. Write it down and distribute the plan to all the players.

If there is any sensitive information involved in the plan, apply some sort of protocol to protect it. *I.e. Personal information, radio frequencies, locations, etc.*

Implement and maintain the plan – now is the time to take the plan for a test drive. This is where you perform a training session to practice the plan. Remember to use the *crawl, walk, run* method to reduce confusion. Do not inject any complications into the training until everyone understands their role. When a problem is found, make note or stop training until it is resolved.

Update the plan as needed – if anything changes such as conditions, personnel, contact information, technology or equipment, update the plan. At the very least be sure to update annually. This formula will help you create the group activation plan we will discuss shortly. Make sure any updates to the plan are distributed as needed and all old copies are destroyed to reduce the possibility of someone using an old version.

As you begin to build plans you will start to see a number of areas that need to be added or improved. That's fine, you should see this.

There is no one plan that will fit every situation. We began with the basics of plan making just to make sure you had a starting point. There is an important key to plan making that you *must* remember: keep it as simple as possible! We know that there is a direct conflict between complete preparedness and simplicity. At this point you should be seeing the benefit of an all-hazards approach.

Plan Annexes and Supplements

Once you have the basic plan built, consider it a framework to improve upon. For a more comprehensive plan there are areas you may want to add. Remember to not go overboard on every plan but if the plan involves a number of people interacting in a sequenced way, they are going to need access to standardized information. An example would be a tactical plan or a convoy plan. To address common information or agreed actions you may want to add what are called *annexes*.

Annexes provide instructions for specific operations. The annex will provide greater clarity and understanding during critical or complex aspects of an operation. An annex is only used if the detail in the original plan was not specific enough to conduct an operation or task. For example, you develop a plan to conduct a patrol. In the plan you address a condition where the patrol sees something of interest and must decide what to do about it. Rather than attempt to write all over the plan with things that may not happen, you devise a standard response at the end of the plan that the patrol can use as a reference in such a situation. The annex will be clear, concise and as brief as possible while outlining all the actions and support available to the patrol.

Here is an *outline of an annex* in operations order format for your reference, fill out any information under these categories as needed:

- o *Situation-* what is going on?
- o *Mission-* what are you here to do?
- o *Execution-* how will you do it?
- o *Support-* who is supposed to help you?
- o *Command and Signal-* who is in charge? How will you specifically communicate with others?

Types of Plans to Consider

Anytime you are trying to keep a number of people organized, it will require planning. Without organization it will be like herding cats trying to get everyone where they belong. Aside from the confusion, there are some very real consequences to not being organized.

Below are some tasks that will benefit from scheduling and planning. In the list below we've included a sleep plan and a mess plan. You must not underestimate such considerations. Why do you need a sleep plan? For the very reason you are in a group in the first place, so someone will watch over you while you rest. If everyone was asleep at the same, who is watching out for threats?

The same goes for eating, bathing, etc. It is vitally important that the group not become lazy or complacent when it comes to security.

An enemy will make all efforts to use surprise to his advantage, it is up to you to deny him this advantage. Additionally, it is not always the human threat you need to worry about. An unattended wood stove, campfire, space heater or candle can lead to tragedy while you sleep. If outdoors, improperly stored foodstuffs can attract all sorts of wildlife. It would be wise to understand the threats and plan for them.

"But I'm Bored!"

Have no illusions, the actual opportunities for excitement will be rare. However, they will most likely happen suddenly and without warning. It has been said by experienced veterans that war is best described as 90% boredom sprinkled in with 10% sheer terror. No one can keep a razor's edge of alertness for long. After a while it seems as if nothing is ever going to happen.

The people that want your stuff will make every effort to be there when that happens. Plan accordingly.

These are some plans that should be considered:

Security plan – A security plan includes a rotating guard shift, the physical security of your location accomplished through careful attention to barriers, perimeters area denial and early warning systems and in some cases a QRF (Quick Reaction Force) to handle threats

Maintenance plan - If you are utilizing machinery or equipment with moving parts it will be important to keep the maintenance up to date. There may not be a parts store available. If using generators, refueling should be accounted for in the schedule.

Be aware of run times and monitor fluids regularly. Oil changes are very important on generators. If you are using battery banks you will want to monitor the charge so as to not completely drain a system. Try to have a way to regularly recharge batteries and monitor loads

Hygiene plan - For readiness reasons you will want to rotate people through the process in shifts so as not to have everyone undressed at the same time and it is good for morale to be clean.

Eating plan – This is also sometimes called a Mess Plan. Rotate personnel through meals so only 1/3 – 1/2 are eating at any one time. Everyone else should be on guard. If threats are near, disburse people while they eat. If going into battle, avoid eating for several hours before, if possible, as gut shot wounds have more complications if the stomach is full, plus it slows you down.

Water plan - Consider where and when to get water. How long will it take to get to the people? Do not run out. For outdoor operations have water onsite for everyone to refill drinking water packs and canteens.

Rest plan – Devise a duty roster to rotate guards. Depending on the conditions, 1-2 hour shifts at the most for late nights. Never allow one person at a time if possible. If he falls asleep… Make sure guards have a watch to monitor the time. Guard roster must be written down to be able to know who is supposed to wake up who and who fell asleep on watch. Everyone should know each other's sleeping locations, so a guard can locate his replacement in the dark.
Waking a replacement is more than a quick shake; *you are not relieved until he is in uniform and at the post ready to work!*

Fire plan - Keep a good amount of wood at the ready. Who is to collect wood? Who is in charge of the fire to keep it lit and under control? Work in shifts to prevent it from burning out or burning you out. Collection of firewood is almost a full time job and it can be hard work. You may need to designate a team for the task.

You can make the response to any threat easier and more effective by considering, preparing and mitigating. This is to say, plan ahead and be ready to act rather than get caught with your proverbial pants down. For our purposes we will say that mitigation can be considered in two ways, mentally through information that removes the mystery of a hazard and how it relates to you, and physically through actual placement of materials and structural reinforcements. I.e. Sandbags for flooding, hardened doors for protection from assault.

The methods and techniques in this book are not fluff or concept, they are proven and in use by groups, agencies and organizations worldwide. Once you accept that preparedness and mitigation are more cost effective and easier than response and recovery, you will be on the way to being truly ready for most anything.

NOTES:

Chapter 9

DECISION MAKING

"Choices are the hinges of destiny."
                                Pythagoras

When it comes to survival, decisions can mean life and death in many cases. Survival is a sudden death game, figuratively, and in some instances, literally. It can be very difficult to choose between multiple bad options, so we need to determine which option will get us closer to our goal of seeing the next sunrise. There are many decision-making methods out there but for simplicity we will discuss only two. There are similarities but a decision made as an individual is approached differently than the decision presented to a group.

Problem Solving – Individual Decisions

An *individual decision* might only affect the decision maker. Should I purify the water I want to drink from this stream? Is that food too old to eat? How can I navigate around that obstacle? These are sample questions one may ask of himself when alone. Ultimately a wrong choice may have a serious impact on that person's survival.

Yes, the argument can be made that if this person becomes incapacitated, it will affect the survival of his or her overall group. In this example the survivor is imagined to be on his or her own.

Whichever method you choose, be sure it moves you toward your goal.

Basic problem solving:

1. Identify the problem
2. Identify options available for success
3. Select best option
4. If no success, reevaluate and select new options until success is achieved.

The above method is objective and almost clinical, but it is easy to remember and it works.

Problem Solving – Group Decisions

Things are different with *a group decision*. In this case the solution will affect others. This is where the presentation makes a big difference. In order to successfully arrive at a decision that affects a number of people, and to get them to participate, you will need them to "buy-in." This is to say that the majority will need to support the decision and endorse the action. For this to happen the problem will need to be presented as it relates to all involved.

Organize the presentation by formatting the problem to include all the pertinent information needed for the team to make a wise decision. Include the timetable and resources available for the task. Identify the nature of the task and what the goals are that would signal success. If there is little time to make a decision, it may not be a good idea to involve the whole team. Differing opinions could take too long. In such a case, let someone with experience make the decision.

This may be one or two people. The more people affected, the more will probably need to participate in order to get the buy-in needed for mission success. This is especially true when the stakes are high and the mission will require group-wide commitment.

Decision Making By Consensus

When voting by consensus, you are effectively working toward compromise. Not everyone will get what he or she wants, but usually he or she will buy-in because they had a say in the decision. Before voting, try to get as much input and discussion as possible from all members. Carefully pair down concerns until you have a fair compromise. Be sure to maintain control of the meeting and keep the stronger personalities from drowning out the weaker members. Try to keep the options to no more than three at a time and use multiple rounds if necessary. Eventually you will be able to whittle the problem and solutions down to something workable.

Also, be wary of *groupthink*. Someone should always play devil's advocate and attempt to be critical just to be sure the decision was well considered.

When it comes to decision-making, try to determine who needs to be involved. When too many people participate, things get delayed, time gets wasted and the situation becomes overly complicated. Make every effort to streamline the process but don't exclude others when a decision affects them. Why? Because you'll risk them not participating in the action that was decided for them if they become unhappy or feel that the decision was reached unfairly.

Gap Analysis And Blind Spots In Your Planning

The best conceived plans on paper are doomed to fail if they aren't rehearsed in varying levels of difficulty. All the planning in the world won't matter if dots are not connected or you missed an important gap in an activity.

Plans are pre-planned sequences of actions that when needed are brought to bear on a situation. If an action cannot connect to another action in the sequence, the plan collapses. So how do you make sure that all the dots are surely connected?

First of all, don't put the proverbial cart ahead of the horse. Start with defining the problem and why it needs to be solved. Next you thoughtfully consider the objective or what it is that needs to be accomplished. Once you understand what needs to be done you set out to figure a way to accomplish it.

When conjuring up a plan you must consider the logistics, the people, skills and equipment that are needed and more importantly, the availability of everything that you need to set this plan in motion. We added availability because often we see plans that are too ambitious for the available resources. This is where things can get dicey, and this is where we usually begin to see gaps form.

What is a Gap?

A gap is a missing dot that is needed for continuity of the plan. Remember the fable "for want of a nail, the war was lost?" A gap is a similar situation. For example, you make a plan to extinguish a fire at the retreat location. A fire breaks out and everyone rushes to their stations. Is there a *working* fire extinguisher? Is the fire extinguisher trapped on the other side of the fire and not close to a doorway?

Another example of a gap involves being dependent on using power tools from home to perform maintenance at the retreat. But, there is no electricity there. Ok, no problem for now, because you have a generator.

For the long-term grid down disaster, you still plan to use your power tools. Do you have enough fuel, oil, filters, spare parts or a maintenance manual to keep said tools and generator operational for an extended period?

The best way to cover the gaps is through working the plan. Practice and rehearse whenever possible. The more important a plan is to your survival, the higher priority it should be given for practice. Our military trains for numerous missions every day of the year in one form or another. After *every* training, after every live mission they get together for a debriefing or an *after action report (AAR)*. Why? Because nothing ever goes perfectly, no matter how much you train. Gaps are exposed and corrected and adjustments are made for *blind spots*.

"There are known knowns; there are things we know that we know. There are known unknowns; that is to say, there are things that we now know we don't know. But there are also unknown unknowns – there are things we do not know we don't know."

Donald Rumsfeld
Former United States Secretary of Defense

What is a Blind Spot?

For our purposes there will be three types of blind spot that can become problematic to the survivor.

Physical Blind Spots

This is the most obvious and refers to the area behind a physical obstacle. Such a blind spot might shield someone approaching our position. An example is a shed that an intruder might hide behind as he advances on your home.

By using terrain to his advantage, an intruder will dramatically reduce your window of engagement against him. He may get too close without being seen in a short period of time. In personal defense circles this thinking dovetails with what is called the *reactionary gap* (the short definition: the minimum distance between yourself and an attacker that allows you to defend yourself)

For the larger type of blind spot you will want to deploy some sort of area denial measures. We like to call them mine fields. Before you get too excited, we can't actually lay a minefield for a number of reasons. For this book, we have modified the concept to achieve a similar result of denying terrain through other *less lethal* measures. When we say mine fields, it indicates they are *mine* to defend; *you* won't be able to utilize the area to your advantage. Such measures of denial may include tactical landscaping with spiky plants, broken glass, sharp metal, a water feature, barbed wire, etc. The idea is to channel people where you want them, and prevent them from hiding from you.

Blind Spots In a Plan

The next type of blindspot is an unknown condition in a plan or activity. You can only plan for what you know or imagine. This is where flexibility and being able to adapt on the fly is important. An example of such a blind spot in planning might be that you have planned an evacuation from an unsafe area; you find that your primary route has been made impassible for some reason (bridge out, chemical contamination, hostile forces, etc.).
No problem, you have a back up plan. Turns out the alternate route is also not practical for similar reasons. Are you equipped to deal with the new conditions?

Do you have chemical protection? Do you have the skills and firepower to challenge hostiles? Can you ford the river? You can only prepare for so many things until it falls on your ability to improvise, adapt and overcome an obstacle with what you have at the time.

> *"The unknowable creates the greatest controversies."*
> Mason Cooley

Fatal Flaws in Decision Making

The most overlooked blindspot is actually a fatal flaw in the decision making process. It is very hard to plan for something you didn't even know existed. This is where myths vs. Facts come into play. If you *think* something is real and true but in reality the information was false or poor intelligence, what are the chances you will make sound decisions in preparing for it?

Are you willing to pay a higher price for success than you should because you really want something? This happens when we allow our judgment to be clouded by pride or haste. Often we use a guesstimate where we should use facts. While there are times when immediate decisions must be made, don't cheat yourself and others with rushed, miscalculated decisions based on emotion or gut feelings just because you *want* something to be so. Back it up with facts.

Remember, survival is often a zero sum situation. There is no way to be prepared for all contingencies. The best you can do is advance cautiously, prepare as much as possible and carefully weigh your decisions.

Detecting Personal Blind Spots

"An unconscious consciousness is no more a contradiction in terms than an unseen case of seeing."

Franz Clemons Brentano

Next time you find yourself in a conversation where the other participant is standing his or her ground on a topic that they live, has personally experienced or has strong evidence to be true, yet you deny, or fail to understand their position, you may have a blindspot issue.

Is it ego, pride, lack of knowledge or failure to communicate that is fueling the problem? An effective leader will find a way to walk it back where such a problem does not jeopardize the task at hand. Of course this goes both ways.

Chapter 10

GROUP ACTIVATION PLANS

"Activate yourself to duty by remembering your position, who you are, and what you have obliged yourself to be."

Thomas A. Kempis

Now that you are familiar with hazards, the triggers that can initiate them, as well as how to prepare action plans, you need get down to the business of survival. Since we are building a survival group, we must figure out how to call everyone together to perform that mission.

A key set of plans that every group must have is how the group activates under different circumstances. How the group musters will depend on a few different factors such as type of event, meeting location (such as primary or fallback) and method of available communication, among other things. You will again need to be creative here. Activation due to a predicted event may not be the same as activation for a severe no-notice event. For example, we would probably have time to react in case of exploding fuel costs and a trucker strike that brings the economy to a halt, but if there was an EMP strike, confusion would ensue very quickly, roads would be gridlocked and traditional communications would likely be nonexistent.

The most important thing to remember is to keep things simple. People have a tendency to skim over plans and *think* they know what to do. Then, when under duress they fall apart and can't remember the details. This is another reason to practice!

I'm not saying you need to stage a complete mock bug-out for the entire group as seen on TV. Given how busy everyone is in daily life, most probably wouldn't participate anyway. But, at least have a solid written plan for everyone to keep in his or her contingency binders. Each member should at the very least practice the plan and keep it current.

Critical plans should be updated and revised as needed and at the very least, annually. Check with all members for changes at each meeting to keep the task under easy control. Notable changes are addresses, phone numbers, email changes, and personnel changes (divorces, marriages, new members, etc.).

When designing plans for activation be sure to consider as many obstructions, physical or otherwise as possible. If you are gathering with your neighbors in your community, your plan will be much different than if everyone is evacuating to a distant location. This applies to both individual and group movements. Much of this overlaps with basic bug-out planning. The emphasis here is in communication and awareness.

Some things to consider when developing movement and activation plans due to an event:

- o Grid outages
- o Hostile areas
- o Restricted travel
- o Traffic gridlocked
- o Convoy separation
- o Contaminated areas
- o Communications down
- o Resupply opportunities
- o Roads blocked by debris
- o Bridges out/chokepoints
- o Primary/secondary retreats
- o Severe weather – ice/snow/flooding

Attempt to look at all the possible conditions members may have to endure in their journey from home to the group muster. It may be beneficial to offer planning assistance and route verification to group members. Another set of eyes on a plan, even though it appears well thought out, may reveal a missed detail and may offer some experience the planner lacks.

There are two common ways to approach activation planning:

We'll see you when you get here

The first method is to leave it to the individuals to figure it out. In this method, the group announces activation and the members follow their self-devised bug-out plans with little help from the group. Keep in mind that some people will not immediately respond to activation for a variety of reasons. They may eventually come but something may be holding them back by choice. It could be family, means, business, illness, skepticism or just trying to collect everyone so the family can move together. This is probably the plan that a widely dispersed group would choose.

We are coming for you

A second method would have the entire group more involved in the activation process. In this scenario group members are more closely located to each other and the retreat or the primary meeting location. A meeting location where everyone musters for subsequent convoy operations to the distant retreat may also be established. If there is a convoy meeting point, be prepared to keep it manned until everyone is collected. If the group is large it might be beneficial to send safe numbers forward in convoy waves while the collection continues.

This period of collection time could be hours or possibly days. Because of the longer wait time, the convoy muster location will require security and sustainment considerations. Choose this location carefully. A mall parking lot may not be the best choice from a security perspective. To expedite retrieval of members, it would be wise to draw a strip map of the area and all members should have a copy.

When a group wide activation is announced, a preplanned course of action would occur. If needed, teams could be mobilized to gather other members and/or other families who need help getting out. This is why the method works well with closely located members. The plans are developed, rehearsed and managed at the group level for efficiency and to reduce poor communication. Alternate methods of off-grid mobile communications will make the process more efficient.

Navigation and the Strip Map

There are no guarantees when it comes to activation. During major hurricanes, floods, earthquakes or impacts, street signs will be gone, trees will be down, landmarks will be missing, buildings may be destroyed and you will not recognize your own neighborhood.

To prepare for a serious disaster event, have every member prepare a strip map. This is a simple, one page map that identifies a location (your home for example) in the center of the paper. Using main roads and durable landmarks sketch and label all items accordingly. Use the top of the page as north and draw a north-seeking arrow. Ideally you will have multiple routes to your location. Try to show an approach from each direction.

The map does not need to be to scale but if there are long sections of road try to identify the distance for added confidence. If there are many identical streets it may be wise to add the number of streets before a turn.

The intent is for this map to assist someone in finding you. Keep in mind that the person with this map might not be familiar with your area so be as complete as possible. After you create your strip map, try to use it or ask someone else to try. This should reveal any problems. Be sure to think about any obstacles and connect the approaches with lateral streets in case of roadblocks. Lastly, write your address on the map so the searcher does not try to enter the wrong house.

Strip Map Example

Once completed, drive the routes and make copies for your binder. Send a copy to the group and/or retrieval team for later use.

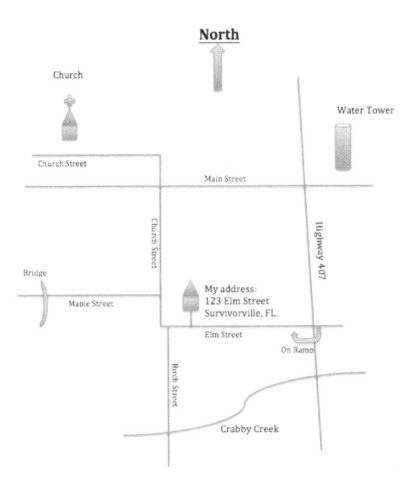

Modify The Activation Plan to Suit Your Group

There is no specific list of activation levels that you must use, but below you will find a framework you can use to develop your own system. You are welcome to use these levels and titles as you your own if you wish. The main idea here is to address the level of readiness or activation at increasing levels of activity.

You will notice that we have included training and self-deployment in our list. This is because we feel that training will enhance the overall readiness and group effectiveness. A training activation level also gives credibility and weight to annual events. Self-deployment will offer members a course of action in a situation where there is no outside contact. This is better than them being left to wonder what to do and doing nothing. Following the list will be descriptions of the terms.

As always, you are encouraged to modify and add to any plan in any way that better suits your needs. All of these plans are just as effective at the family level as they are at the community level. We encourage all families to use similar planning and processes as the group at large to create an air of familiarity and understanding among all members, this includes children.

Most importantly, keep it simple, easy to remember and use words everyone understands. Make every effort to standardize terms and definitions in all plans to reduce confusion.

Sample Levels of Activation
o Normal operations
o Training
o Enhanced readiness
o Mobilize to primary
o Mobilize to alternate 1
o Self deployment

Normal Operations

Normal operations refer to the condition of daily life. No specific concerns observed. All members continue routine activities and regular meetings. Continue to train and improve preparations as per plan.

Training Activation

A training activation is called when the group wants to test responses and plans. This could be an announced training exercise or unannounced drill. Try to not trigger too many unannounced practice drills or it could drive people away from the group. It can also cause friction when people are too busy to participate. These work well when planned with everyone's schedule in advance. A summer camping trip would be a good time to try this out.

Enhanced Readiness

This level of activation would be used when there is a potential threat to daily operations. Potential triggers would be a serious geopolitical event with homeland repercussions, severe incoming weather, a major economic event, pandemic issue, large-scale blackout or anything else that should be monitored. In this condition

The group would make final plans to activate the group just in case. Members will top off supplies and be ready to move to the retreat location. All family members will stay in close contact and family contingencies should be reviewed and any changes passed around as needed. All members should be contacted through the communications plan for accountability and participation confirmation in case the group needs to activate. Apply span of control measures to prevent missed communication items.

Mobilize to Primary

This order is given for a real activation. If communications are still operable, use the call roster to contact everyone. Use your activation code words if desired for security. Attempt to confirm eta (estimated time of arrival) for each member and confirm that they are planning to join the group so you can watch for them. Some people may choose to not participate for various reasons. Some people may not be able to mobilize. By checking accountability, you can decide if a team needs be deployed to pick up members in distress. This also gives you a general idea of what the headcount is and what skills may not arrive. In some cases members may need to evacuate on foot. This means that you may not see them for days or even months depending on the distance traveled, so make sure you've planned for these delays.

Mobilize to Alternate 1

In case the primary retreat location is out of service or the route to that location is impassable, you may decide to fall back to an alternate location. If this has been decided, *make absolutely sure that everyone is aware of this*. Whether the alternate is in the neighborhood or many miles away, everyone needs the information somehow. Contingency messaging should be addressed in the Commo plan. If the group or family has a secondary alternate location, the same methods should be used. The command in such a case could simply be "Mobilize to alternate 2".

Self Deployment

In extreme cases where communications have collapsed and the situation appears to require evacuation to the retreat, members may need to make the decision to mobilize without being told.

Potential triggers might be a nuclear strike, an EMP or a major cyber attack where infrastructure and communications are paralyzed. For fellow survivors located in other countries without reliable communication systems, such an event might be civil war fighting that abruptly moves through their area, civil unrest or a severe natural event.

In case of self-deployment, the member should follow the agreed group plans first. There may be interim meeting locations or message drops where you can meet others before moving to the retreat. If you are located near other group members in such an event, you may want to try to find them before committing to a long haul journey to the retreat, especially if you don't know what everyone else is doing or if the retreat location even exists any longer.

If you do move toward the retreat, attempt to leave messages at your *home* or *pre-planned* drop points along the route for other members to find. This is also helpful if convoys become separated or plans change.

The key point to remember about planning for contingencies is to keep things simple. Focus on immediate priorities while still preparing for the long term. Most importantly, communicate and practice, practice, practice. Even when the big group is not together, members should keep their preparedness up to agreed levels, and their skills sharp. A family is a small survival group. If the families are ready, the larger group has a better chance to be effective in times of crisis and survival.

Chapter 11

COMMUNICATION WITH MEMBERS

"The single biggest problem with communication is the illusion it has taken place."
George Bernard Shaw

As with any type of organization there should be a way to reach everyone to dispense information, request a status update or initiate an activation order. A proven method is a telephone roster or *call tree*. This is a living document. Information should be updated as needed and at least annually. It is recommended that contact information updates be an agenda item at each meeting. When a list is revised date rather than revision number for ease of understanding should identify it.

When developing a call tree be sure to limit the number of calls any one member must make by spreading the workload. There are a couple of reasons for this. By using a top down call order, a key member should only need to call a few people. If there are levels of leadership, just follow the chain of command. This will simplify the process, prevent duplicate calls and ensures everyone is called.

The system also has a major benefit of keeping everyone involved on a regular basis. By establishing key group/team leaders, a member can reach out to the next level key member with any questions without calling everyone in the book. In this model, information flows both ways in an organized fashion. Think of it as a flow chart. It is critical that key members be reliable and available. Try to limit the number of calls to 3-7 per person.

Impress on the members the importance of completing their calls.

When adding contact information, be sure to include the primary contact number, then alternate contact numbers, and then other forms of communication such as email, online messaging or radio call signs. It is also a good idea to annotate whether a member prefers a text message or does not text at all.

A call list will not work if members are not available. It may be a good idea to have members, especially key members, let the call leader know if they are going to out of contact or away on business so an alternate can be tapped in case of an activation. To verify the call tree, hold occasional drills to reveal any gaps or weaknesses.

Call tree tips:
- Keep an updated contact list
- Assign reliable key members to make calls
- Keep initial call message clear and brief
- All call leaders should convey the *exact same message* to prevent confusion down the line
- Limit the number of calls per person
- Don't count on messages being received, call again
- Keep a record of who answered and who did not
- Report back upward of any non-contacts
- Test the call tree occasionally
- Have the call leader reach out to lower levels to verify they have been reached during drills (spot test)
- Write down any questions when clarifying for a member
- Consider using an out of state contact as a group wide information relay in case of local or regional communication outages (long distance lines usually work when local lines are down) be sure to let that person know the tree is activated

o Make sure the relay has the latest updates in case someone calls

Be sure to build the call tree into your *communication plan*. Here is an example of how to organize a call tree:

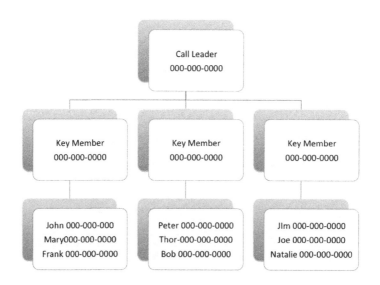

This is just an example. When you design your call tree be sure to add all the contact information for each member. This is a sensitive document; make efforts to keep this information private. For those desiring increased security, the information can be altered or coded. Some groups may wish to take added measures to compartmentalize the list by separating the components among teams and never keeping all info on one document. To do this, only give a key leader the contact info for his or her small group.

NOTES:

Chapter 12

PLANNING AND HOLDING MEETINGS

"An association of men who will not quarrel with one another is a thing which has never yet existed, from the greatest confederacy of nations down to a town meeting or a vestry."

Thomas Jefferson

All groups operate at a higher level when they hold regular and productive meetings. This is important for ongoing group maintenance, developmental reasons and especially for collective tasks or projects.

Beginning with normal operations, let's understand why and how meetings are so important. In order to be effective in a team format, people need to spend more time with each other. This bonding time creates the environment to learn each other's behavior, how members think, their body language and what is important to them. Lines of communication are opened and honed, and relationships are developed. This should lead to an increased commitment to each other and the group as a whole.

When meetings are irregular or not given much priority time begins to slip away, important decisions are delayed and progress grinds to a halt. Also keep in mind that when members don't see activity, they lose interest. To avoid such problems, determine a meeting schedule as far in advance as is practical. One method that works well is to come to an agreement of which day of the week works for everyone. For example, Tuesday may be good. Next determine the frequency of meetings. Most people are comfortable with a monthly organizational meeting. One of the easiest schedules is to remember is to pick a week of the month. So now we have decided to hold a meeting on the first Tuesday of every month. Simple. No dates to remember, no confusion, and plenty of time to plan ahead as far as the calendar can see. These monthly meetings are the official "we strongly suggest you attend" type meetings.

In today's busy society it is difficult to be everywhere we want to be. For this reason some groups hold several monthly opportunities for education, training or fun. If you go this route try to offer a couple of weekday classes and some weekend classes to mix it up. The idea is to give members plenty of options to be as engaged as they want and also to give those members who are always busy, a more flexible schedule.

One group we spoke to finds success in offering two field-training opportunities each month. One is usually daylight training and one is overnight. Combined with the various classes throughout the month they seem to have good regular participation. They have also formed a mutual agreement with neighboring groups to train each other's members for even more flexibility. All members should try to participate when they can, but these additional gatherings usually are not mandatory. It is important to not make the group too intrusive in our everyday lives. I like to say that; "we don't live to prepare, we prepare so that we may live." Too many events will burn people out and cause friction. Another thing to remember is that usually, 20% of the people do 80% of the work in any organization.

Handling No-Shows

We are going to circle back to our discussion on carefully selecting members here. Everyone gets busy; there will be some turnover. Many groups have what are considered their *core* members.

Then they have those that loosely participate due to other obligations. You will need to decide if the rare participant is worth keeping on the roster. This may be a good agenda item for a meeting. Then there are the members who were initially there but have since fallen to the wayside for some reason. When called upon they usually have a reason they can't make it, again. The group would be wise to investigate prior to dumping them.

Contact the member and inquire if there was a problem with another member or how the group is being run. Issues such as these can usually be fixed by methods in this book. If the member seems to be less interested or has no solid reason for not participating, perhaps he or she has lost interest. Sometimes financial ability or transportation is a problem and they don't wish to discuss it. Remind them that the group is there for each other and offer to help get them back on track.

Some groups have a rule that if you miss a predetermined number of meetings, you're out. This may be too harsh for your group and that is ok. There is no universal requirement here. Every group will be different.

Conducting Effective Meetings

Meetings may be the only time members can receive direction, share information, make decisions and coordinate tasks. In order for all of the above to happen, a meeting must be organized, on track and productive. As we continue, we will identify the characteristics of effective and poor meetings.

Poor Meeting Characteristics:
o No agenda
o Missing personnel
o Start and finish times not met
o Time wasting is not controlled

- Too much focus on pet projects
- Participation limited due to someone dominating the meeting
- Run-on meetings become boring
- Breaks needed from uncomfortable conditions such as bad chairs
- Poor behavior disrupts the meeting
- Poor follow-up on previous meeting items and decisions causes loss of action, or waste of someone's efforts

Effective Meeting Characteristics:
- Meeting leader outlines the meeting goals, time allowance and expectations
- Leader initiates and maintains focus on the agenda
- Leader ensures that all decisions are understood in a clear way.
- Members leave the meeting with a clear understanding of what was agreed on.
- All members respect each other's opinions and strive to keep meeting productive
- Minutes are kept of all discussions and decisions
- Meeting ends on time

Meetings that are structured will run more effectively and in less time. No one wants to participate in open-ended meetings that only seem to involve certain parties. Likewise, a two-hour meeting that only pertains to a representative of one department about 10 minutes in total will be a waste of his or her time.

"Take advantage of every opportunity to practice your communication skills so that when important occasions arise, you will have the gift, the style, the sharpness, the clarity, and the emotions to affect other people."
Jim Rohn

Participant Roles in a Meeting

There are five roles suggested roles in formal meetings. It is suggested that instead of these roles emerging on their own, that they be assigned and rotated for subsequent meetings. This will work to keep people involved and aware of what is going on. The roles are:

1. *"The facilitator"* – chairs the meeting
2. *"Time keeper"* – keeps the meeting on schedule
3. *"Secretary"* – records the minutes of the meeting
4. *"Devils advocate"* – this person is responsible for critical examination of any ideas proposed to prevent *groupthink* from emerging. The last thing that a survival groups wants is to miss out on potential gaps and blind spots because the desire for harmony or conformity results in incorrect or deviant decision outcomes.
5. *"Team players"* – everyone else involved in the meeting process

The Meeting Agenda

To keep a meeting on track, have an agenda prepared in advance. If you are not sure what to discuss, begin with open items from the last meeting, move onto current issues then something fun or educational. It is also helpful to reach out those who may be in leadership positions to see if they have something to discuss before the meeting.

Keep in mind that it is not appropriate for a subordinate member to surprise everyone at a meeting with an important topic for discussion during a meeting. Such items should be organized before the meeting with the leadership and placed appropriately on the agenda.

Conversely, if a meeting topic turns into a long drawn out discussion, it may need to be pulled back to examine the purpose of the topic.

It may be necessary to stop the discussion and assign a committee of a few people to hammer out some options so that a vote can be more easily made. If the topic is time sensitive, the group doesn't have to wait until next month to vote on it. Call an interim meeting or, if possible, use one of the free online voting/polling programs available on the Internet. If, of course, the Internet still exists.

It is always a good idea to add something educational and/or fun to a meeting so they are not always boring. Just be sure to not waste people's time. Start on time and attempt to finish on time. If a topic is too big and a resolution cannot be accomplished, you may need to table it for now and gather further information or break it into smaller pieces as we discussed earlier but get the meeting done or people will lose interest. The goal is to have everyone leave a meeting in harmony so problems don't fester until next time.

If possible have a meal before the meeting and/or dessert after the meeting. Meals help to promote communication and gives everyone an opportunity to catch up with each other before, rather than during, a meeting. Dessert and coffee after a meeting encourages people to stick around for a little while they digest what was accomplished in the meeting and encourages suggestions for future events while it is still fresh in their mind. Meals together help people bond and establish relationships. This is an important part of building loyalty and commitment to each other.

Besides, who wants to pass up a chance for someone else to cook?

Chapter 13

NEW MEMBERSHIP

"I knew that my vocation was found. I had received the call, and having done so, I was sure my work would be assigned me. Of some things we feel quite certain. Inside there is a click, a kind of bell that strikes, when the hands of our destiny meet at the meridian hour."

Amelia E. Barr

One of the most important processes the survival group will ever undertake is granting membership. There are several schools of thought on the subject and there will be those who attempt to downplay the importance of vetting new members. Sure, it may be hard to find the right people. For instance, you may be limited to what is near you, with the only alternative being to go it alone. Sometimes it is what it is, there is no denying that.

But, first of all let us be clear on how a new member can help or hurt the group. Throughout this book so far we have identified numerous opportunities where a person, family or clique could do irreparable harm or injury to others in a stressful or dangerous situation. Bad attitudes spread like an infection that can send a group into a dysfunctional tailspin. Mutiny is a big word but it is very possible if the right characters are allowed to hold the group hostage when things don't go as they please.

How bad would it be to invite someone who may be a felon, rapist, thief or pedophile to be in direct contact with your family? This is especially dangerous in a world without law. Besides, by the time you discover the bad apple, something bad may have happened to make you aware of that person. Do you want to put loved ones in that position? Aside from this, what if they are lazy, demonstrate extremely poor judgment or become a burden in some way? These are the harsh realities when social order has broken down.

This book is designed to be used as a reference at all levels of group existence, from the sole individual trying to decide if a group is right for him or her to the well established survival community. At any point in that spectrum, a bad apple could place a lot of people at risk. This is not to say potential candidates should be polygraphed and cleared top secret, but due diligence will save tremendous headaches later on. It is always more difficult to eject people than it is to admit them.

Just remember that you may have to live with the decisions you make when it comes to inviting people into the family, or putting your family with other people. This reveals another concern. Family members. We can usually choose our friends but we are assigned a family. This doesn't mean we naturally have to like them. Every family will have members that just don't fit. I will again remind you of the annual holiday dinner party.

Family includes those who have married in, their children and the potential misfortune of uppity in-laws. Tough choices will have to be made here. If you are reading this book during a time of peace, now is the time to have that conversation with everyone in your circle. Don't come off as apocalyptic, overbearing or crazy. Be prepared with factual information. Avoid nebulous, unfounded statements and wild claims; just make a good case for why working together makes sense. It is certainly essential to convince the spouse of any group member why this is important.

A spouse who can't understand why the other half just blew three years of vacations to buy assault rifles and survival food will cause severe problems within the group. Just apply some common sense conversation to see where they stand on the issue of preparedness.

I recommend that you do *not* give yourself a stroke trying to change their views. It will not work, it never does. If they are not interested just refocus and use stealth training on them to foster natural change or write them off. Harsh? Yes, but that is the way it usually works. They will only change when they want to. Hopefully it won't be too late where their sudden change of heart ruins all of your careful planning and other survival relationships.

In order to convince people to come around to your way of thinking you must be able to make a solid case and back up everything you say with facts and levelheaded responses. If you lack credibility or make wild claims based on something from the Internet, you risk losing that person's respect very quickly. Remember, this way of thinking may be very different from how a person may have been raised. You are pulling people out of their comfort zones and asking them to prepare for something they may have never seen or even heard of. It takes time and care.

Women in the survival group

"All places where women are excluded tend downward to barbarism; but the moment she is introduced, there come in with her courtesy, cleanliness, sobriety, and order."

Harriet Beecher Stowe

A quick look at organizations and populations with high numbers of younger males compared to females will show historically, increased violence against outsiders or other groups. We have all seen this from families with many sons to sports teams to military units and even families where the mother has not been present.

There are some groups who have sworn off women from participating because they feel that over time feelings may change and relationships will be contested. In a survival group the dynamics among the members are essentially exposed every day. The men and women are always together doing the same tasks.

One could see where each gender group is exposed and almost easy to compare in the eyes of another. Envy, jealousy and protective behaviors can become an issue. All the same issues we face today will be amplified in stressful and very close living conditions.

This is not to say that having women in a group is a bad idea, as a matter of fact it would be a poor survival decision to not include them. It is best to find a way to keep the drama and gossip to a minimum. As a note, men are just as susceptible to such behaviors we just tend to gloss over things. Feelings can't be helped and the best way to keep such problems under control is to build as solid a group as possible and keep everyone working toward the same goals. A strong sense of community combined with respect and honor will help.

"A mother-in-law and a daughter-in-law in one house are like two cats in a bag."
Yiddish proverb

It should be expected that relationship and generational differences would at first be a big problem.

Everyone will have an opinion on how to best proceed or how to perform some kind of task. In contrast, apathy or lack of direction can just as easily cause friction. Just as in today's society stronger women will have a role in establishing order. There is no established rule to prevent squabbling other than to try to remind everyone that the situation requires everyone to participate in the group's interest and to try to understand this is not the perfect situation. Everyone will need to be less critical and more engaged in the job at hand.

The best advice I can offer when it comes to hostility among members is to treat the situation as a nuclear detonation: Time, Distance and Shielding. Diffuse the situation by separating the members; give them some time and space to relax. After a while it will be important to find out what the real problem is and address it. There may be no real problem other than frustration in which case it will be an easy fix. If the problem is serious or happens repeatedly, corrective action will need to be taken. Left unchecked, minor issues can become major problems. This is where clear rules that were well considered at the group's design will again pay off.

"People who work together will win, whether it be against complex football defenses, or the problems of modern society"

Vince Lombardi

Individual v. Centralized Thought

Throughout this book you will see there are some parallel threads of thought for you to choose from. One thread maintains individuality as a member or family unit maintains most of the responsibility for their own existence. The individual or family enters the group with many of the skills and supplies with the potential ability to make it on their own for an extended period of time. While desiring to remain independent they also realize that there are benefits to being part of a collective. The individual will participate in the collective for the betterment of their little community and in turn, the betterment of their survival situation.

Not too distantly separated is the concept of a more centralized system. This is common for larger and more organized groups where all members become a more integral part of the group. In this concept everyone works to strengthen the group. All resources are invested and all supplies are distributed as needed. When members arrive all their food is collected and stored in a central location along with food from the other members, though other survival and personal supplies may remain with the individual. Meals are cooked from the inventory by designated cooks and served communally. The reason for this is to keep everyone fed and prevent bad feelings if someone shows up without their supplies in hand. The goal is to switch to food production onsite as soon as possible and save the pantry supplies.

Perhaps we could analogize this concept to Durkheim's *Functional Theory*, which states that all values are shared and the group adopts a living organism-like function where everyone has a place in the small society. As nice as the theory sounds, it is difficult to pull off when there is diverse membership. It is important to communicate the goals and reason for combining supplies. Remind those who resist that they too may lose all their supplies and show up empty-handed.

The survival group will most likely end up being a little of both styles if you have good leadership and solid members.

If not, then it may end up resembling a social group/homeowner's association. Don't let that scare you away. Both groups have their pros and cons it's just that the cons are usually more visible than the pros. There will be disagreement, gossip and electioneering that is just the way it is when you bring strong personalities together. It doesn't help that a diverse crowd of survivors will usually have various firm beliefs in what the future holds and how to prepare. Add in some religion, military backgrounds and socioeconomic diversity and the process can be somewhat turbulent until effective leadership gains control. This brings us back to the issue of careful selection of membership and clear mission statement.

So how do you build your survival dream team? We have touched on the basics throughout the book for things to look for and pointers for talking to people. Let's sum up the process.

The Individual Perspective

Begin with looking inward as an individual to answer these questions for yourself:

- What is it you are looking for from a group?
- Do you have any medical issues or disabilities that could limit your participation?
- Do you plan to stay with a group for the long term?
- Are you planning to move on in time to another location away from the group?
- Where do you want to end up?
- Are you willing and prepared to relocate?
- What are you willing to compromise on?
- What are you not willing to compromise on?
- What do you have to offer a group by way of skills or materials?

- Have you truly considered what to do about family and friends?
- Are you responsible for children or anyone with a disability?

On a side note, some information will be very private in nature. All members should be afforded the highest levels of confidentiality. If a group is aware of any pending medical, background or personal OPSEC concerns, care should be taken to prevent public disclosure without the member's consent. With this being said, it is strongly suggested that all members make the group aware of any of the above concerns that could adversely affect the organization. This is especially true of preexisting medical issues. Given the nature of a survival group's operations, medical surprises in a remote or austere situation could have devastating results if not accounted for. It is in your best interest and for everyone's safety to help others to help you. Do not count on the highest quality of triage and medical care in such an environment.

Finding Group Identity

The existing group will have many things to consider prior to opening up to new members. Here is why having a set group identity is important. If the group does not have clear goals, it cannot effectively build its team. Imagine what kind of potential candidates might show up if you were vague in your existence. Yes, they will show up because they will know about you from your existing members. Lets say you plan on being a family oriented homesteading group. There will be those who will associate such an honorable endeavor with a militia group. Careful vetting and explanation of group goals can mitigate this.

It must be made clear what the group is *not* about to all existing and potential members.

This step can help to reduce dissatisfaction when all the group does is talk homesteading and does no tactical training that a member thought they would see.

By answering the following questions, the group will have a strong, consistent message to present to potential candidates. Remember, these people are interviewing the group just as the group is considering the new member. If the group is sloppy in its presentation, it will be obvious to the candidate. Just as in the business world, you will want to attract the best people and weed out the rest. Answer these questions as a group before meeting with a candidate:

- How often will the group meet?
- What are the group's overall goals?
- Is there a membership goal in mind?
- Is this an open group or a closed group?
- What is the process for adding new members?
- Will all family members need to be vetted or just vouched for by candidate?
- What baseline membership requirements will the group establish?
- What will the group do if a solid candidate does not yet meet the baseline requirements but has a desired skill?
- What is the process for ejecting members?
- Is the group open to members outside of the local community?
- How long should a member participate in "public" meetings before being admitted to the retreat location?
- What form of leadership is in place?
- What is the process for selecting leaders?
- Has the group determined a desired list of skills?

- Which skills are missing in the group and how bad do you need to acquire them? Can they be learned or must they be found in a candidate?
- Does the group need any specialty equipment?
- Does the group have a retreat location and how many people can it support?
- What will the group *not* tolerate?
- What, if any, financial arrangements will the group work under for group projects?
- What image does the group wish to portray? (families helping each other, community assistance, religious based, militia styled, etc.)

You must know who you are and where you are going if you expect people to join you for the right reasons.

Establishing Baseline Requirements For New Members

To reduce the strain on a group during an actual activation, it may be desirable to require members maintain a certain amount of supplies. For example, some groups will select a period of time for food stores. The common requirement is one year but some groups realize how hard it can be to achieve such a goal and will start new members out with as little as two weeks with the goal of increasing their stores in time.

Notably, there will be a problem with verifying that a potential or new member has the required supplies. Very few people are interested in being inventoried and rightfully so.

The group has a couple of options here.

1. The group can provide a space for members to secure a certain amount of supplies at the retreat and the rest at their homes to demonstrate commitment.

2. The group can make a rule that in case of activation, the member must show up with the required supplies to sustain his or her family, or have a good reason for not bringing the supplies such as destroyed or contaminated, etc. Note: if you have ever attempted to move a years worth of food, you will realize that it won't be easy or quick. The task may require several trips or a large trailer. Plan for this.

3. The group may take the members word that the supplies are a priority and are actively being procured to increasing levels.

Usually those who lose the ability or interest in adding to their supplies will also start missing meetings. It will become obvious in time, who has lost their way, so don't sweat the supply issue too much. This is another reason to not rush new members into the group or reveal private information. It is not unusual for the process to take several months to formally accept a member.

At the end of the day, the reason for such measures is to give the new member a goal and to keep them on track with preparedness. When a member is not thoughtfully admitted to the group there may be problems later. No one wants conflict but if a member loses steam on preparedness and too many other things begin to get in the way, what will happen if the group activates? The people that took this seriously are going to be upset at having to carry people that showed up with little more than an appetite and their *year's* worth of food.

When considering what a new member should bring to the table, think about what the group is preparing for and how it might need to live in the aftermath.

For example, if the members live in a tsunami prone area, they may need to leave within minutes but may only need to survive as a group for a couple of weeks until shelter can be sorted out with family or friends. In such a case members may not need a years worth of food but a solid bug-out plan and supplies would be sufficient. If a group were planning for a major pandemic, then a year supply of food and survival equipment would be a good idea. If the group is preparing for whatever may come, a year or more of supplies and sustainability skills may not be such a bad idea to have on hand.

As you can see, the mission goals of the group will help to identify the supply levels and type of personnel a group may want to consider. Just keep in mind that if the group becomes too strict in their requirements, there will not be many candidates that can meet the entry requirements.

Mobility - Another Angle To Consider

Remember that this is a survival group, and the very nature of a survival situation may force the individual or group to move or keep moving. In such a case it won't matter how much food one has stored, it may not be possible to take it with you. For this reason I would suggest that a baseline of supplies *begins* with mobility in mind. True preparedness runs on simultaneous tracks. The survivor must always be improving his or her current position but at the same time be prepared to walk away. This is to say, while you are preparing the home or retreat to shelter in place, make plans to immediately evacuate.

What would happen if you built a fortress of food and supplies and the place caught fire? What if Mother Nature chose your location as ground zero in the next big production disaster?

What if a bigger group decides they prefer your place to theirs? If this happens to the group retreat it could deal a great blow to everyone. For this reason I suggest that part of new member baseline preparedness include *realistic* bug out supplies, skills and planning. Part of such planning will undoubtedly include designs to move young, elderly and disabled personnel. For these reasons it is important to consider very carefully the type and quantity of supplies that each member have ready on very short notice.

What do I need? The evacuating group is just a bigger version of a family on the move. We all know by now that the more you know, the less you need.

With this in mind, think back to the 7 areas of survival, with the addition of *transportation*.

- Food
- Water
- Shelter
- Safety/Health
- Security
- Communication
- Energy
- Transportation

This list is modified in scale because you must be able to walk with these items. Do not count on any mode of transportation other than your feet and even then be on the lookout for an alternative.

When building the bug-out bag be honest with your skills and abilities. Focus on the life safety items from the major categories and worry less about others.

What do I mean? Think climate, water, food, first aid and self defense first. If possible add communication and transportation.

If everyone can provide the basics of survival for themselves, the group will be better able to focus on the problems along the way. This will also be important if anyone gets separated or weather turns foul. For these reasons, follow the scuba diver's rule #1: "Everyone carries their own gear".

Without getting too far off topic, when traveling by vehicle in an evacuation scenario, keep all bags closed, shoes on the feet and be ready to bail out at any time. This goes for kids too.

To sum it all up, try to get all members prepared to shelter in place at the retreat location for the minimum prescribed period of time (1 month, 6 months, 1 year, etc.) while simultaneously working to get everyone ready to walk away with only what they can carry. Think about where the group would go, how far it is and how long it might take to get there on foot. As you can see, there are plenty of things a group can do to remain active and have fun.

Good Candidates, Inadequate Supplies

Given that this book is a reference for multiple scenarios we must address what to do when a member or candidate is unable to present the required level of supplies. In such a case the group may need to provide for the member and his or her family to have the benefit of a specialized skill. In other words, you may want to make an exception for the right person until that person can get up to speed with his or her preps. It will be wise to have a procedure for such an instance in advance. When might this happen?

It may be more of a possibility than you might think. An example might be that a group has been recently developed or perhaps an event just happened that presents an opportunity to form a group.

Catastrophic events sometimes happen with little notice and may even destroy hard earned supplies. Another example might be where a person, family or another group arrives at your location with little but a desire for a place to stay. There are obvious dangers to admitting strangers to your group but circumstances may dictate choices in a disaster. In certain cases it may be beneficial to consider what a person can offer a group in exchange for a place to stay. We don't have to remind you of the potential dangers of such an agreement, as evil comes in many forms.

Just be careful in accepting unknowns into your perimeter. You may want to follow that gut feeling about people. If your sense tells you that something is not right, it may be a good idea to move on. Gut feelings work on the back burner of the brain by combining many pieces of information that the conscious mind is too busy to see.

Vetting Potential Candidates

"The trust of the innocent is the liar's most useful tool."

Stephen King

When it comes to considering new members the group will want to attempt to get a complete picture of the potential candidate if there is time. Of course if this is a "come as you are" situation you may need to make some judgment calls.

When time is on your side try to have a comfortable sit down interview/conversation in a comfortable, neutral location. A quiet coffee in a diner or in a walk in a park where you can take the time to get the candidate to relax usually works well. There is a strategy that has been shown effective and that is where the group sends out an investigation team to visit with candidates. Usually 3 current members will meet separately with a candidate who was nominated by another member. If this is too intense for your group, feel free to conduct your investigation however you feel is appropriate. The reason for separate meetings is that each member can get a feeling for the person without convincing each other in some way.

Some groups prefer to use a questionnaire with a lot of questions. This can come off as very strict and may turn off a good candidate. Many groups are moving away from such things preferring to make an interview more organic. In this way they just have a conversation and see how things go. Don't be a speed dater, be genuine and remember to give and take.

Another thing to keep in mind is that most people can keep up controlled behavior for a short meeting. This is why police officers used to make people wait for about 20 minutes after being pulled over for DUI before questioning them, in time the adrenaline begins to subside. Now of course most departments have breathalyzer kits. Try to chat for at least 30-60 minutes if not more. This can help the candidate to relax and begin volunteering information about themselves, their family and their views on different subjects. Remember, you may need to live with them in the future; it is worth taking some time to be comfortable. In a true long-term survival situation there will be a lot of down time.

It would be good to know how to speak to a member anyway. Actually meeting potential candidates that you really want to include is a pretty rare occurrence so don't worry, this won't be a common task that takes a lot of time.

Take care to not turn the interview into an interrogation and don't make it feel like one by bringing the candidate before a panel of members. All you are trying to accomplish is to get the candidate to relax enough to be honest about who they are as a person and what they believe in. As we have said previously, the candidate is interviewing you as well, so be on your best behavior. Don't ask private questions or anything you would not be comfortable answering yourself. If the candidate has family, you may want to ask them to join in because they will certainly be coming along if things go bad.

The more likely situation where you will be talking with a potential new member will be a social event. Remember back when we discussed where to meet people? You won't want to spill the beans too early in a relationship or to someone you just met. Get to know them for a while through some social engagements. If no events are scheduled, invite them over or have your existing group get together but don't advertise that you are a group, just have a barbecue or watch some sports. Any pleasant atmosphere will do.

There should be no indication that everyone at the event is part of a survival group. When people hear the word group, they react in different ways. After the social event, ask each other what they think about the prospect. If there is favor, proceed slowly and chat the new guy up for while. By a while I mean for several occasions to be sure you have a comfortable picture of who he or she is.

Once everyone agrees that this person may be a good fit it is time to open up about the group. Contact the new prospect and see if he or she is interested discussing it.

The conversation and following questions are in addition to the questions we posed earlier in this chapter regarding what the individual is looking for in a group and what the group is looking for from a potential candidate. It may be a good idea to create a discussion sheet so you don't forget to ask something important. By the way, since you were careful in the first meetings, you should already know about any extreme feelings with regard to religion, government, race or politics. If these areas concern you and the candidate feels too strongly in any of them, you may want to cut that person loose before you go any further. The deeper into the process you go, the more you have to risk.

If you have decided that the person or family is worth interviewing, here are some additional primer questions to ask after the pleasantries. Try to make it a comfortable conversation but let them know how serious you and your group take this process.

- Have you ever thought about taking preparedness to another level?
- Would you be interested in being part of a group of friends who prepare together and would be there for each other in case something happens?
- What would you be looking for in a group?
- Is there anything specific you are preparing for?
- Would you commit to joining our regular meetings and any events we host?
- What concerns would you have about being in such a group?
- How many people would you want to bring into the group? Family, friends?

- Are those people on board with emergency preparedness or do any of them think it's silly?
- How is your preparedness going? Are you moving forward in collecting supplies? Skills?
- How long do you think you might be able to survive with your current stores?
- Without being too prying, try to get a feel for any debt load that may stall the candidate's progress. (If this concerns you)
- What kind of skills do you have and how long has it been since he or she actually tried to use them?
- Do you have reliable transportation and time to participate?
- Is there anyone you would not want to participate with you? Neighbors, family, etc.
- Is there any concern or any disabilities that may become a problem in an active environment? What is the health of the candidate or family?
- Has the candidate been in a group previously? Why did they leave?

While chatting with the candidate look for personality cues that may offer insight into his or her personality:

- What is the person's temperament? Do they seem overbearing or timid?
- Do they have extremist views or views that contrast with the group's stated goals?
- Do they appear to truly be interested? Are they just along for the ride? For instance, is one person extremely interested and their spouse is bored or seems agitated.

In many cases you won't have the luxury of finding the perfect candidates. We understand that every group and situation is different. The above strategies are intended to be a guideline to develop your own admission process and to give the reader perspective when applying to a group. At the end of the day, the group will just need to decide if a person is a decent fit, and the candidate will have to decide if the group offers the safety and security desired. If the attitude from member or group seems to indicate the following; "Sure come on in, we'll be bunker buddies while the world burns" you may want to continue your search elsewhere.

Stolen Valor

"Three things cannot be long hidden: the sun, the moon, and the truth."

Buddha

A note on a topic near and dear to my heart. There is an unfortunate trend of people claiming to have served in the military when they have had no military experience whatsoever. Sometimes they may have actually served but embellish their claims of awards or experiences. They usually do this to receive accolades and benefits. Many have found out the hard way that true veterans have no patience for such fraud.

If a candidate or anyone associated with a potential candidate claims to have served it would be wise to have one of your real vets sit with them for a little while and have a nice conversation to get a feel for the person and figure out if they are telling the truth. It won't take long for the fraudster's story to collapse under a few well placed questions by someone who has been there.

Civilian Background Checks

Some of the better-organized groups choose to perform background checks on potential members. Sometimes this happens in an oblique fashion in one of the funneling sources we discussed at the beginning of the book. Sometimes they choose to run a criminal search. Either way you would be well served to make sure that the person you are considering is not a felon or sexual offender, among other deal breaker offenses. Don't be too quick to dismiss this step. There will be women and children in the group. They trust you to provide for their safety.

Trust But Verify

Even after you have decided to give someone a try, you may want to make sure they are willing and able to walk the walk. All the conversations in the world will do no good when survival requires dirty hands. We have all met the armchair survivalist who learned everything by Internet video and is now an expert, or the mall ninja who has all the coolest survival gadgets. Neither of these people is usually proficient in such things.

My caveat is this: if you are sincerely interested in learning but aren't yet completely proficient in a skill, I'll gladly help. If you think you know it all and are untrainable due to your ego, I can't help you and don't need you on my team. Survival in its truest sense is not a video game or Hollywood movie; there is no room for showboating or the imagined warrior. I believe in the old adage *trust but verify*. If you are still on the fence about the new candidate, take them out on a test run by going to the range or camping for a weekend. If your group has a class coming up invite the person or family along. Anything that gets the person out of his or her comfort zone will reveal how they adapt to non-everyday conditions.

More importantly, it will demonstrate their ability to play well with others.

If you really want to see what someone is like under pressure, take them canoeing. Nothing will test a relationship like a two-day canoe/camping trip. Well, short of having a child with them, but that seems excessive at this stage. I've always said that if I were a divorce lawyer, I would set up a kiosk at the end of a canoe run.

Potential Problem: People Knocking On The Gate

Assuming the group is activated there will be people making their way to the retreat location. There will be a mix of members and refugees. One idea to handle requests for entry is to print a list for the gate guard. The list will include names of people who have been approved for entry and a list of skills that the group has decided it would like to have.

If your name is on the list, you get to come in. If your name is not on the list but you have a needed skill you may be given an opportunity to come in for an interview. Some skills are important enough that people without any supplies may be granted entry and membership. For more information on desired survival skills, see the directory of skills in our earlier chapters.

Refugees that do not fit into either category may be turned away. Special consideration may be made in cases of injury or special hardship. For example, if parents with an injured child arrive, they may be admitted for basic medical help then sent on their way.

If a member shows up at the retreat with extra people that were not accounted for, the group will have to decide how to handle this.

There is no easy answer but, if you turn those people away, the member may leave as well. However you choose to deal with this problem, if it actually is a problem, may likely invite conflict of some sort. The best way to handle it may be to sit the involved parties down privately and discuss how things work. Let them know they can stay if they respect the existing roles and rules of the group. They must participate in whatever capacity is asked of them and understand that by being here they are in effect taking food and supplies from the mouths and hands of others. As we discussed earlier, everyone needs to be an asset to the group.

The member should know this and avoid placing the group in the uncomfortable position of having to judge whether or not to admit the people with him. They should all know, if this arrangement were not acceptable to them they would be asked to leave. Make sure they are clear that once they agree to the terms and conditions, they become subject to all the same rules and possible ejection as anyone else. Once they are integrated into the group, they will need to be trained up in any areas deemed necessary and helpful. Be sure to consider any limitations or exceptional knowledge they may have when deciding where to place them and what to train them on.

A note of caution to the member who fails to prioritize and comes up short on doomsday. If you have been finding every reason to avoid stocking up on supplies and show up empty-handed and the group is aware of this, they may not let you in the gate. Most groups fully expect that some members will lose control of their supplies or be forced to leave their supplies behind in the aftermath of an event. This is part of the planning process discussed earlier. But, if you have chosen to purchase that big screen TV while claiming poverty when it comes to food storage, you will probably be on your own.

You must establish your priorities when it comes to preparedness. It takes time, money and effort to put yourself in a good position and those families that have struggled for years and done without won't take too kindly to being forced to share with someone who has procrastinated unnecessarily.

Chapter 14

GETTING THE NEW MEMBER OFF TO A GOOD START

"You can discover more about a person in an hour of play than in a year of conversation."

Plato

One of the worst things we can do to a new person is to shake hands, point him to a bunk, and walk away. This person has been accepted as essentially a member of the family and should be introduced properly. Since a survival group is not all that dissimilar to any other multiple member organization, it is safe to continue the teamwork theme we have thus far embraced. There are some common complaints that people who are introduced to new positions regularly share. Frequently they are dumped into a position, overwhelmed and left to make or break right away. Often times because everyone else is too busy, the new member is ignored or bored.

Either way the new guy may become confused and not be productive. This is not his or her fault but the older members may translate their first impression of this person as not useful. First impressions are very hard to change. First impressions go both ways. Poor induction problems can drive a new member away, and that can have all kinds of ripple effects for the group.

A well-organized group will have the new member team up with a sponsor member. The sponsor will escort the member around for introductions and explain how things work. This is an important first step that will clear up any confusion about how things are done. If a meal is planned, be sure to include the member and don't let him or her sit alone. If the group is not activated, have the sponsor remain in regular phone contact to keep new people interested and let them know they are welcomed and cared for. Have the sponsor personally call the new member with invitations to training opportunities.

Due to security reasons there is no need to share important information just yet, for now allow the member to get settled in. There will be plenty of time to integrate the person further into activities and plans later. As of now there will be more than enough for the new member to do, we do not want to overwhelm him or her. Part of the goal for now is to keep them interested and coming back. Keep in mind that getting to know each other types of exercises can and should be done regularly even if there is only one new member. Only time will tell if the choice to admit the new person was a good one.

After couple of visits have an official welcome for any new members. This may be a good time to perform the oath with the group so the new member truly fells like part of the club. Continue to check in on him and see how he is adapting. Don't forget about the family, their support is a very important key to the success of the new member. Be sure to invite them to all meetings and plan activities that the whole family can enjoy.

Chapter 15

RESOURCE DISTRIBUTION IN THE GROUP AND BARTERING SURPLUS

"The value of a dollar is social, as it is created by society."

Ralph Waldo Emerson

When a survival group comes together many things will need to be worked out. As we discussed earlier, the members will come from different backgrounds and will certainly have differing viewpoints on how things will operate. One of the biggest hurdles to get past will be allocation of resources. It will be difficult enough to get members to participate at agreed levels due to many reasons. Not all of them bad but some people just do not have the resources to all at once to meet the required level of supplies and training. Conversely, there will be those who seem to be very prepared and have the skills and supplies to be self-reliant for a very long time. It kind of sounds like everyday society doesn't it?

Skills v. Supplies: Which Member is Better?

Where the conflict arises is how do we attract quality members with skills to offset the members who have the financial wherewithal to be well supplied but may lack the skills to survive when things get dirty and sweaty. In order to combat this, do we combine all the incoming basic load supplies into a common storage system? Or do we have all members remain responsible for their own basic load of supplies? What happens if they are short? Will they be ejected? Are we supposed to open our hard earned larder to feed those who were unable

to plan in time or perhaps chose to chomp through their food? What about medical supplies?
Everyone forgets about those. One traumatic bleeder can tear through a pile of supplies. Then what? These are the tough questions that must be answered.

Remember in the beginning when we discussed why we were joining the group? It was for mutual support in tough times. You will notice an overarching theme in this book. It is one of trust and commitment. This is another reason it is so important to carefully consider and vet any members, you may at some point find that you need to share your supplies with them. So with this all being said, the easiest way to move forward may be to establish base line supply requirements. We will go further into this subject later.

Individual v. Community Supplies
If your group chooses to work in the fashion whereby each family or member is responsible for his or her own food supplies, you can further break the discussion down to what would be considered community supplies. Just because these supplies are labeled "community", does not mean they are automatically forfeited to the group leadership.

One possibility is that, for example, Johnny brings an unusually large or specialized piece of equipment such as a large hospital tent, this just means that it would not be necessary to duplicate this investment at this point in time. The same can be said for tools, chainsaws, generators, vehicles, etc. In this way the group can allocate funding in other areas since the equipment is present for use. How and who uses it is up to the owner of course, since he made the investment. A potential downside to this arrangement would be if Johnny decided to take his stuff and leave the group. It is recommended that such a concern be addressed and redundant equipment is allocated based on stated priorities.

Rule Refresher – Stealing and Community Resources

Even though everyone is allegedly here for mutual support, there may come a time when things come up missing. We already touched on this in the rules section but as a refresher, be sure to properly secure all food, valuables and bartering supplies. When people become hungry or disillusioned, they may take things or eat someone else's food. Unfortunately, people are people. Some want the easy way out and some will attempt to save their own supplies for an emergency while taking advantage of others. Such actions could be a big problem in a stressful survival situation.

Depending on the group makeup, there are a couple of ways to handle resource allocations. The following methods are not written in stone. Feel free to adapt to your situation.

Situation 1: The Diverse Group

If the group is diverse with several or many families, it's highly recommended that everyone bring a baseline set of supplies. Members would be responsible for their own food stocks and feed themselves. Medical supplies and personal equipment can also be maintained within the individual families. If there were a need for additional supplies by other members, it would be up to the family to decide whether to share.

You should think very carefully about sharing your individual resources with other members. There may come a time when you desperately need something from another member, but what if the other member doesn't remember the favor? This is where trust is so important in a group setting. Another option is to barter within the group but what do the other members have to offer? Additionally, if a member owns a specialty item or tool, it might be in his or her interest to be the operator of the item rather than loan it out to be returned broken with ill feelings soon to follow.

There should still be community production efforts such as agriculture, water collection, firewood collection, etc. Community efforts should be divided fairly with respect to distribution.

Situation 2: The Big Family

If the group is one large combined family you may be able to combine the supplies and designate cooks to prepare meals for everyone. There are many similarities to the diverse group but this group will more resemble a real family with communal meals. This group may still include family friends that are not blood relatives but are very close. We all have memories of that dysfunctional Thanksgiving weekend with family. Just because we are all together for the important reason of survival doesn't mean everything will sail along smoothly. Families are people too and we may not like all of them but they are here anyway.

For these reasons it is still a good idea to secure everything, especially food. Do you really trust that brother in law to not enjoy a late night snack at your expense? It is a tough world if the group finds itself together for survival and everyone needs to be clear on the boundaries. Fences make good neighbors. Padlocks on a pantry help with that.

Just as with the diverse group, you will have communal tasks and production of resources. It may be more difficult to get family to participate with chores, just because family rarely likes to take orders. Even so, crops, meats and other sundries should be doled out fairly and evenly.

Sustainability and the Group

Whether your group is one big family or a makeup of several families, it is important that you become sustainable as soon as possible. It may be a surprise when you see what that really entails. This is all the more reason to not wait until the world falls apart to get started. Always keep in mind that in order to keep your team strong, you will need to provide for their needs. Some needs are physical and some are psychological, either way, they are needs.

Remember when we discussed customer service early on in this book? You (almost) can't have too much abundance but you can starve to death. Next we are going to help you turn that abundance into currency.

Surplus Supplies and Bartering

Survival is far more than wandering the hills eating plants and bugs or living in a bunker until the war ends. There are extremely few people who can live a totally self-contained life without outside help. Even the most rugged of mountain men must ride into town to trade their furs for supplies or purchase feeds, building materials, parts, tools, etc. Our goal as a survival group is to create a self-reliant community of sorts. We try our best to gather the skills and supplies that would best further our days above room temperature. The skills and supplies we don't have, we must get. By adding members we hope to complete the circle that allows us to live as we choose without the need to look outside. But there will always be something that we need.

Since this book is about the worst-case scenario, it is important to realize just how much we would need in such a world. As we said before, we are not going to dive into all the numbers and statistics of what it takes to survive. That information is already written in many places. You are strongly encouraged to study and at least understand the basics of nutrition as it relates to differing survival environments.

In a nutshell, you will need at the very least, 1200 calories per day, and if you are working the hard life of a farmer or soldier, that number moves upward of 3000+ calories of properly balanced nutrition. That kind of nutrient intake will be very hard to maintain long term by eating only stored foods.

There are plenty of books on the market that will tell you how much garden one would need to produce per person. It would be wise to over estimate and go as big as possible to account for failure or unforeseen disruptions.

The reason we say all of this is to get you to think in the surplus. If you need it you will hopefully have it. If you have extra, you may be able to barter with neighbors or in a community somewhere. In a world where food is in short supply, having extra may be better than holding precious metals. The trick to bartering is to establish a fair value of the items in hand. For example, a basket of fresh vegetables may be an even trade for a slab of fresh meat. A day of labor may be a fair trade for a couple of meals. If you are operating a farm as we discussed earlier, you may have an entire harvest of vegetables and maybe a surplus of meat to trade.

If a group is located near a farm they may make an arrangement to provide labor and security to the farmer in exchange for food. Although some groups we spoke with didn't seem to give the impression that they would take no as an answer from the farmer for this cooperation. There are other trade items that may be stocked by the group for barter such as fire making items, water purification tools, clothing, and vice items such as liquor or tobacco.

We are not going to discuss bartering in depth but there are some things we suggest you *do not* do. It is never a good idea to trade ammo, weapons or other dangerous items with strangers. It is also not a good idea to offer toxic or contaminated food or equipment to an unwitting trade partner.

Bartering Safety Tip

We want to add a tip that we haven't seen or heard anywhere else on the topic, and that is to be aware of those interested in trading to only see what you have. This is a security problem. Think of it as a possible probing attack. If someone demonstrates an interest in bartering but just can't seem to decide after you have shown him everything you have to trade, it may be a ruse. What you may have done by showing off your surplus in yard sale fashion was to indicate what you are worth. If a seemingly innocent conversation drifts into your other areas of survival, the person may be sizing you up as a target. It may be enough to give him a reason to attack, kidnap for ransom or take your stuff in some other way.

Don't underestimate people, those that have the gift of gab are good at getting people to open up and share too much. To work around this potential problem, decide what you are willing to barter and bring only a few things. Act like it's all you have and there isn't much more where that came from. Remember there are times to look just as desperate as everyone else. Avoid looking like you are well cared for. Almost no one wants to rob the homeless guy, they prefer the well-dressed guy flashing all the good stuff and talking too much.

The Charity Plan

We need to touch on the topic of charity. Even though it is labeled as a plan and should also be considered a contingency, we added it under the bartering and surplus section. The reason for this is that you need surplus to offer charity or you will be operating under diminishing returns pretty quick. How you will deal with charity is a topic that should be considered early on. Many groups build it into their initial planning and some identify it as a goal early on in the group design.

Why is charity such a big topic? Remember where we talked about human nature and some of the reasons that members may decide to not join the group in real world activation? One of the most popular reasons we hear is that they can't leave other family, friends or neighbors. Even at the group level there will be someone in your sights who may be starving, be it an elderly couple, a child or someone disabled. The group will have to decide what to do in this situation.

The Stray Cat Syndrome

If any of the above scenarios presents itself, the last thing you might want to do in a time where food is currency is to openly feed outsiders, unless you have the ability to keep feeding them. Why? We've all seen it. It starts with the one little cat that seems to particularly like your driveway. It's cute, it's adorable, it's without help, and surely it wouldn't be too much to put out a little can of food for it. It doesn't cost much money and it makes you feel like you're helping the community. Have you ever noticed that on day 2 suddenly there are 3 or 4 cats in the driveway? The numbers add up pretty quickly. The same can be said for openly feeding strangers. Word will get around that your group has food and you are willing to part with it. Not only do you run the risk of running out of food for your own family as the number of "helpless" individuals increases, but you've also made your group vulnerable to attack because neighbors will soon learn that your community is thriving.

A solution to help the less fortunate comes in what is considered the truest form of philanthropy: anonymous charity. This is where the beneficiary receives help but doesn't know where it came from, and you (and your group) as benefactor aren't telling anyone either. If the person(s) needing help are neighbors, a care package left anonymously overnight on their step would accomplish both of the goals of assistance and anonymity.

A note of caution! Sneaking around in the dark when people are prepared to shoot first and ask questions later may be a bad idea. Take your safety into consideration when trying to get supplies to others. Charity can breed goodwill for the group if performed carefully and safely.

Protecting Your Investment

As with any currency, you will want to provide the proper level of physical security and operational security to keep people from trying to steal from you.

The beauty of operating such an enterprise is that the abundance can provide for protection and in some cases, power. Since food may be currency, it can be used to purchase other resources or even information. There will always be someone who is willing to share what he or she knows to better their position or fill their stomach. Just be sure to trade fairly so that relationship doesn't backfire on the group.

Chapter 16

THE GROUP AND THE OUTSIDE WORLD

"Alone we can do so little; together we can do so much."

Helen Keller

There is no way to know what societal situation you will be in as you read this book, but it is likely that the world still exists in some form. For this discussion we will operate under the assumption that the group has activated, things are bad and there appear to be darker days on the horizon. You have formed a group for mutual protection but as we observed earlier, it is very difficult to meet all of your needs without interacting with those beyond the perimeter.

Subtle Changes in Society

If the societal situation has not devolved into total anarchy and there is still a civil system in place, there will be social interaction between your members and everyone else. Just as we all have our daily pre-disaster lives with jobs and responsibilities, it may remain this way for some time in the case of a slow downturn. Not all disasters or collapse events start with a bang. Most of the time there are a number of slow burn problems that culminate into catastrophe. During this period we must all interact with others in our endeavors.

A valuable observation for today and tomorrow is that we are all poor at a different level. When our individual resources drop below our personal requirements, we are in trouble. No matter who we are.

History books often skip the lead up and instead offer more of a headline approach to notable historic events. Even if there is plenty of data available, most people will skim through and jump to the end, drawing unfair conclusions as to what went wrong to cause such hardship. Unfortunately this fuels the mentality that the entire system will collapse in almost overnight fashion.

While that could happen, it hasn't yet. There were always a series of lead up events. Hidden in these events is where things seem cloudy as to the direction things may be headed. Also hidden in these events are the challenges of survival. One of these challenges is our interaction with others that are in the same boat. We will all have to deal with the same problems if/when society changes. Remember the old saying that everyone is poor on a different level. While sounding ridiculous, it does carry some weight.

Keep this in mind during encounters with other people and remember that your neighbor down the street might one day be more than just the guy you wave to at the mailbox.

Insiders and Outsiders

First, a little about behavior among established group members and how they see the outside world. It doesn't take long for those who band together to form bonds. Depending on the situation the bonding can take as little as two days or upwards of three weeks. The more intense the scenario, for instance, post doomsday where daily survival depends on teamwork, will speed up the bonding process. An interesting thing happens as a group bonds.

As this happens, the members will begin to disassociate from outsiders.

This is not saying that a group will become abusive of non-members but there is the potential for this to happen as isolation and competition for resources continues. Leadership will need to watch for such animosity. If a situation develops where the world has devolved into rival gangs, such behavior could lead to battles for power. If the world were showing an opportunity to coexist, the group would benefit from outside contact and possible commerce.

Building Relationships and Gathering Intel

Just as survival is a holistic endeavor, you will see recurring themes in many of our chapters. One of those themes has to do with interaction with nearby communities. It will benefit the group to cautiously interact with neighbors for supplies and information about happenings in neighboring areas. A note of caution, one must always be wary of rumors. Remember that rumors have a tendency to grow as they spread through the community, but in some cases rumors begin from an actual truth.

The more avenues of information you have available, the more ways you can verify information. One such avenue would be to remain in contact with, and in the good graces of, local law enforcement. It may be a good idea to even have members of law enforcement active in the group.

The goal here is not to be that mysterious cult-like group in the woods. We all know that in the absence of information, people will manufacture their own views based on nothing. Complete isolation can be a bad thing for the group as throughout history it has been shown that people attack that which they do not understand.

To form beneficial relationships with others, one needs to find out how the two can help each other out. In the case of a farm, a friendly gesture of a homemade product to the local patrol might be a good start. Of course never reveal important group information to others, but being on the friendly side of the local population is a good thing. The goal here is to remove any mystery surrounding your existence while inviting others to share news with you.

An example we are all familiar with would be from our childhood. Do you remember the "haunted" house or the mysterious old man that no on ever sees? There was probably no basis for such stories yet they stood the test of time. At least until the old guy turned out to be a nice grandpa and the haunted house was painted, cleaned up and sold to your new best friend.

One group that was interviewed shared with us, that by offering home cooked meals and pastries to local patrols they were able to harvest a relationship to hear about any information of incoming upper level agencies or increased crime in their neighborhood.

It turned out that the group was not alone in its quest for survival in the region. Knowing that there are others working a similar mission in your area is an important piece of information. However, bear in mind that if things ever get really bad, people will self-censor to keep from drawing attention to themselves, or they may spread disinformation.

Establishing Mutual Aid Compacts With Other Groups

"The best weapon against an enemy is another enemy."

Friedrich Nietzsche

Much in the same way an individual will benefit from aligning with others for survival, the same is true for groups. We spoke several times thus far about the need to reach out to others for materials and skills you don't have. Remember the mountain man who makes his way into town to barter or trade for supplies? The same holds true for the survival group.

While such a group should arguably be better prepared for most contingencies there will always be something the group will need by way of skills, assistance or supplies. This is especially true in the early stages of group development. In time you may have a complete community but given the possible economic or societal situation in which you find yourselves, you may find yourselves in need of some form of support.

There is no telling where this book will find you but rest assured, there will be people somewhere within walking distance from you, maybe even too close. First and foremost you must attend to the overall security plan. It won't do any good to open up to others if they become another threat to your safety. Just as you carefully and cautiously admitted members to your group, you should be just as careful when handshaking with another group.

Friend or Foe?
Each Group Is Different

One thing to keep in mind at this point is the other group is a wholly separate group from your own. They may not share your goals, values, ethics or interests. They don't have to, that is why they are the other guys. This doesn't necessarily make them the enemy, but you will want to know where you stand with them. If it turns out that your two groups suffer from irreconcilable differences then at least you will be aware of the problem. If this turns out to be the case, adapt your security plan to keep an eye on them. If it turns out that they may become hostile, create a contingency plan to deal with them.

If another group, family, camp, etc. Seems to be friendly it would still be wise to proceed with caution. This is where your intelligence network comes in handy. If the other group is open to the idea of mutual assistance, offer to work together to develop a contingency plan in case trouble arrives in the area. Be sure to adapt both Commo plans to better signal for help.

At the very least, the group should be very aware of their neighbors, no matter how distant. It would only benefit the group to know which groups are friendly, and which groups are not. People who currently live in remote areas understand the importance of mutual aid. They may not get together and play cards every Friday night, but if the situation turns dire they understand the value of working together. The better your network, the more opportunities you will have by way of commerce, intelligence, medical care, defense or even the mundane, such as a rogue cow escaping in the night.

Neighbors are not the only group that may be available for mutual support. Faith organizations such as churches would be a good place to start looking for networking opportunities. Take a moment here to reflect on the goals and values of your group. If a church or religious group aligns with your stated goals then you may want to participate in their activities. By doing so you will become familiar to the members. As we discussed earlier, familiarity helps people open up to you.

Isolation can work against you. How you desire to be perceived, whether out in the open or isolated, is up to you. Just remember to move slowly in relationship building.

Safely Negotiating With Others

It is wise to make efforts to understand another's motivations for your own *safety and potential benefit*. We say *safety*, because the desperate will seek your weaknesses to their benefit. We say your *potential benefit* because the more you understand others, the better position you will be in to negotiate a deal.

Deals are always best negotiated from a position of strength. Strength comes from knowledge, position and having something that someone else wants. Being able to parlay that something to your benefit further strengthens your position.

As an aside, be careful in your dealings be it with another group or individual. If the deals are lopsided or winner takes all type deals, it will foster distrust and resentment on the loser's part. If things are already so bad, why make the situation worse by taking unnecessary advantage of others? Such dealings will eventually come to haunt you. Try to remain fair and honest in your dealings with others.

Have a Designated Negotiator

You might be surprised at how often a good negotiator can be used. Anytime there is an opportunity for trade, cooperation with another group, disagreement, threat or even kidnapping, it would be good to have someone to act as a mediator or negotiator. Negotiating/mediating is something that can be done with outside forces as well as within your own group. This person will be able to speak on your behalf and even collect intelligence on the situation through contact with the other side if needed. As with all things survival it would be a good idea to designate a back up person who can assist or replace the lead negotiator.

In order to conduct effective negotiations there are a few guidelines that should be followed. You must enter the negotiation with a complete understanding of what you have to offer, what you desire to receive, what you will not agree to and what you might be willing to compromise on.

One of the keys to successful negotiations is trust. The other side will be more likely to make compromises if they feel as if they are getting a fair deal and that the person making the deal is authorized to speak on behalf of the group. Once there is a handshake, the deal must be done. The person you select must have that authority and integrity to follow through. It only takes one bad deal to destroy a relationship. If things are bad you will want to improve relations not make more enemies.

As you can see this may not be a task for just anyone. You may just expect that the leader would always conduct any talks but that is not always the case. In fact it may not be wise at all. If the stakes are high then perhaps you will want to send out your leader, but anytime you do this you elevate the talks just by doing such a thing.

The other side may see that you went straight to the top, which indicates you consider the talk to be higher in value. Besides, if you send the leader out and he is incapacitated or kidnapped, where does that leave you? Save him for later in case talks become more important. A point to consider is if they send out their leader, you must decide if you should do the same so you don't insult them.

If you are perceived as insulting, you may need that alternate negotiator sooner than you expected. It may be wiser to begin the negotiation with a trusted representative who is well spoken, well mannered, trustworthy and knowledgeable in what is being discussed. Use someone who does not come off as threatening if the goal is to inspire cooperation. If the goal is to instill fear in the other side then send someone who fits the bill.

Whichever way you go, the negotiator must understand that the message should be clear and well understood by the other side. If terms cannot be immediately reached back off to reconsider if negotiations are even possible, rather than allow the meeting to devolve into a drawn out shouting match. If you are speaking from a position of strength you should have time. Use it to your advantage and let the other side think on it. They may just need time to realize their own position.

If time is of the essence then you are probably not negotiating from a strong position. This is where it is especially important to know what you will do and won't do before you start talking. Sometimes people panic when they are against the wall and cave unnecessarily and lose more than they should have. A strong negotiator will help you in such times.

It is important to make sure you communicate to all members that no one should ever make deals or arrangements or speak on the behalf of the group if not authorized.

There should be one point of contact for all outside discussions. If a deal or situation comes up that affects the group at large, the member should bring the information to someone who is in charge or authorized to make such decisions.

Be Clear When Making Agreements

When making deals or agreements be sure to be very clear in your understanding of what is to be agreed on. Never leave details of an agreement to the imagination, do not be ambiguous. When both parties walk away there should be no room for confusion. Survival is a serious game and do-overs are rare.

If you and another group agree to support each other in some way, don't walk away from the table by just agreeing to support each other. What does that mean? Will you each have bumper stickers made up that say, "Support your local survivors" or did you agree to send your men into a firefight on their behalf?

These are the kinds of details that you'll want to know, and you'll need to make the entire group aware of in case the agreed upon scenario actually takes place. The last thing you want is to make a deal with a neighboring group and then surprise your own members with a "by the way, we agreed to send them 1 cow for 3 goats."

Find Common Ground

There is no specific answer to every contingency but it will benefit you to know what you need and what you have to offer. When hammering out some sort of support agreement, attempt to discover what the two groups have in common. Be sure to consider what problems are common as well as what solution both groups have to offer. For example, both groups may have a defensive problem.

By understanding any weakness in the areas of defense, a plan can be formulated to work together to increase the safety of both groups. Why would the other group want to work on a similar goal? Because if one group falls, what will prevent the other group from suffering a similar fate? What about resources other than firepower? One group has a good supply of vegetables; the other group is doing well with livestock. We all know that food will be among the most difficult resources to keep on hand. Other trade agreements will be found in the list of desired skills we discussed earlier in the book.

Mutual aid compacts need not be limited to strictly emergency support situations. Over time such agreements can and should evolve into commerce and community alignment. Take the problem of transient population.

If a community can come together in support of each other, the impact of pass-thru traffic on a group's location can be mitigated. We are not saying to set up a farmer's market right away. That might backfire, because if things are bad, word will spread quickly about a place where people can go to be fed and protected. The fledgling system could be overwhelmed in no time. Community building is an ongoing process that takes time and patience.

Training Compacts

We covered this in the training section but it is worth repeating. In peacetime it may be beneficial to invite neighboring group members to train with you and vice versa. This will build solid relationships and trust. It can also keep members involved by offering more flexible scheduling of training opportunities.

Chapter 17

RECOGNIZING AND DEALING WITH OUTSIDE THREATS

"Every man, in his own opinion, forms an exception to the ordinary rules of morality."

William Hazlitt

There will most likely come a time when the *group* is forced to deal with an exterior threat. In the hazard analysis and contingency planning sections we discussed how to identify and plan for threats, but what are some tactics to recognize such a threat? For this chapter we will focus primarily on *the human hazard*.

People will always be your biggest problem

Throughout history we have seen countless examples of people attempting to take advantage of each other. From one-on-one assaults to global wars, humans are a violent species. We don't need a global collapse to see how people might act towards each other; the answer is obvious in our daily lives. It is recommended that the survivor make efforts to gain an understanding of why people behave in a certain way.

As you are building your library, look for books on human behavior. One such book I recommend is The Lucifer Effect by Philip Zimbardo. Dr. Zimbardo created the Stanford Prison Experiment. The Stanford experiment is another eye opener into human behavior that is highly recommended reading.

In The Lucifer Effect, Dr. Zimbardo attempts to understand why good people turn evil. This is relevant to the survivor because most of us are good people, but if we are forced into a survival mindset, we may find ourselves doing bad things to others.

Our survival as individuals, families and groups will depend on our will to survive and the levels of behavior we are willing to accept. Survival is approximately 90% mental and 10% everything else. As we see in society today, there is a widening gap of class separation and there is an undercurrent of public distrust of government not seen in ages. People are widely different in their views and in very many cases; people don't see a problem at all. Both perspectives are problematic to our situation as pre-disaster survivors. As we explore some behavioral issues you will come to learn some clues to look for and patterns that indicate trouble is brewing. But first, let's meet our adversary.

Risk Homeostasis

A popular topic among social researchers, many professionals have performed studies that directly apply to why people seem to ignore or discount danger to themselves. These studies seem to shed light on another phenomena we see everyday in emergency preparedness: Procrastination. So why do people essentially gamble with their own welfare and in some cases, their lives and those of loved ones? Why do people wait until the last minute before stripping a store bare ahead of danger? Why do some people seem content to stick their head in the sand when there are alarms everywhere saying danger is near? People tend to let their preparations get lax due to a concept called *risk homeostasis*.

Risk homeostasis refers to the idea that in any activity, people accept a certain level of risk to themselves regardless of the true danger. It could be a risk to their health, their safety, or anything that's important to them. However, they also know that the particular activity will benefit them in some way. On a daily basis, we as humans compare the level of risk with the amount of benefit that we are going to receive. We as survivors observe that the goal is to minimize the amount of risk, while maximizing the benefit we're going to receive.

If the level of level of projected risk appears low, then we're willing to take the risk that we'll receive a huge benefit. *If the level of projected risk seems higher than the projected benefit, we're not willing to take the risk.* In translation, this describes the people who say things like this:

- "Bah, I've been through 13 hurricanes. It's never that bad, I'm not leaving" (then they find themselves trapped in an attic when the levy breaks)

- "The water doesn't look too deep to drive through. I think we can make it" (vehicle washes off road, family drowns, happens all the time)

- "The government will take care of me if an emergency happens" (then they go on TV blaming FEMA for not being there with food on the first day of an event)

- "I'll wait and see if things get worse before I go to the trouble of getting ready. We have plenty of time." (Then they stand in endless lines for supplies at the last minute, complaining about the line)
- "I'll never need that generator again, the storm was a freak occurrence" (they sell it online shortly after the storm because it was taking up space in the garage)

- "I don't need to use my new survival gadget until a real emergency so I'll keep it stored away" (an emergency comes and said gadget fails when it was needed most or they have no idea how to use it properly)

- "I have lots of guns, ammo and body armor. If it gets bad I'll take other people's stuff" (my kid could shoot you in the ear with a .22 leaving your kids as orphans. Think marksmanship. People who have stuff, usually have the firepower to defend it)

- "I don't need to prepare, I'm coming to your house for the apocalypse" (no you're not)

Risk homeostasis is that strange place where the mind either ignores some form of danger or subconsciously attempts to compensate for it. It's one thing to allow this to happen to yourself but when you are the family leader and kids or a spouse is depending on you, their lives are in your hands.

So how does this become a threat to you? In every one of the above scenarios the person or people that chose to not be prepared or took their chances and lost, could be on your doorstep or in your path at some point. Their desperation could become your problem. It may not be an outright confrontation, but they could force you into an ethical decision that could have safety repercussions for everyone.

Behavioural Mimicry

This is a term used to describe the behavior that people display when they are around other people. Babies learn to mimic facial expressions; gang members mimic similar gang behavior. Mimicry does a couple of things.

Through imitation a person flatters another, which in turn fosters acceptance, which then reinforces the behavior mimicry. Over time, the behavior, whether good or bad, sets the standard to be built upon either in a positive direction or a negative direction. There may not always be a positive reason for mimicry; often we do not even realize we are doing it. It is natural human behavior.

It fills the need to be a part of something bigger than we are as individuals, such as a survival group. (See what I did there?)

Through training and bonding, mimicry can be a positive force in the group. Why is this important to understand? Because it is a part of what we call *mob mentality*.

Mob Mentality

"The most dangerous creation of any society is the man who has nothing to lose."
James A. Baldwin

Have you ever seen a group of people make some really bad decisions that they would probably never make as individuals? We've all watched the news and seen groups of seemingly "ordinary" people participate in gang assaults, civil unrest, vandalism streaks, and the destruction of public and private property. These are examples of decision in numbers, going with the flow if you will. It has been shown that a reason for such group behaviors is that the group provides a level of anonymity, a place where the individual can act out with little danger of being identified or caught. In many cases the individual is encouraged to act out. This can be an enticing escape from a world of rules and laws.

Mobs can form for many reasons but there is one condition that will draw a serious mob faster than others, that condition is hunger. The inability to feed one's family will cause people to get off the couch. Politics, religion, civil rights and social issues regularly draw people together in protest and there may be some violence but if you mess with the food distribution process, violence will increase.

Food insecurity is a condition where people are not sure where their next meal will come from or they are undernourished. This is not only a 3rd world concern; Americans are currently experiencing a severe problem with food insecurity. A stunning 20% of children in the US do not know when the next meal will come.
Record numbers of Americans are on some form of government assistance. Food manufacturers are compensating for profits by shrinking packaging sizes yet keeping costs the same, for now. Many children have poor nutritional habits due to foods that are cheaper than healthy.

Our food distribution system has come full circle and now creates the same conditions it was designed to prevent. Only now we are starving with stomachs full of junk rather than just having empty stomachs in many cases. Immune systems need proper nutrition to stave off illnesses. When children lose access to regular meals, protective parents will act to feed them at all costs.

The Thin Line Between Good and Evil

When people are placed into dramatic social and environmental situations, their normal human behavior can be transformed from good to bad. Actions that were once considered taboo or morally distasteful eventually seem to be an option. This is true of most everyone. It takes strong character to avoid such a trap and even then the descent to primal behavior can be so subtle you don't recognize it until it's too late, if ever. People will adapt to their situation regardless of social or ethical norms if they are pressured enough. Eventually it becomes easy to justify deviant behaviors when you feel as if your survival depends on it, whether that is true or not.

We say this because the long-term survival group will greatly benefit from employing and enforcing normal societal structure and systems to stave off such behaviors among their members. Without such standards, people will become victims of their circumstances. When confronting the difficulties of a survival situation the group must strive to adhere to the goals and values so carefully chosen at its inception.

By not recognizing the new societal situation of a long-term event, the group members may eventually succumb to the laws of the jungle outside the gates of the homestead. In such a case, the group may find itself imploding under its own weight. At this point the group will either dissolve or fall under some sort of tyrannical leadership.

It was observed in <u>The Lucifer Effect</u> that good people could be induced, seduced and initiated into behaving in evil ways. Because of this they can be led to act irrationally, mindlessly, and will be self-destructive and antisocial when immersed in *total situations*. Such a situation would be conditions that challenge the sense of stability, consistency and individual personality of people. What this is saying is that situational temptations can induce good people to do bad things. I.e. Hungry people will steal or worse.

The condition can be made worse through the social mimicry we spoke of earlier and the potential narcissistic behavior of a strong group. Studies have shown that when people bond together in a group, even if they began as strangers, they shortly become aligned to each other and will demonstrate a higher level of suspicion and hostility to those not in the group, whether the outsiders were aggressive or not. The group leader will want to keep an eye on these potential problems.

Left alone with little structure or management, people will take advantage of weaker or contained personnel for their pleasure and entertainment. This has been documented in the Stanford experiment and more recently with the detainees at the Abu Ghraib detention facility in Iraq. It only takes a situation where one group objectifies another for abuse to take hold. History has demonstrated this when a soldier has testified, "I was only doing my job." Or "I was ordered to do it." This is something to take note of when contemplating if troops would fire on their own countrymen.

If the group finds itself in a situation where prisoners are detained, be sure to establish strict rules of care and supervise all guards closely. Potential problems will arise from immersion into a bad situation. In many legal cases it has been determined that the situation, and the seeming approval of leaders provided the conditions for normal, intelligent people to become abusive and dangerous to those under their care. From an exterior threat perspective, it is not a stretch to think that strong leaders could even convince weaker personalities to do the unthinkable if those weaker members feel it will improve their standing and care.

Such conditions in a societal collapse could create large numbers of gang members who desire to secure a regional "turf". If your retreat is in that area, a confrontation could be in your future.

Moving From a Hardship Society To A Tactical Perimeter

Now that you have some insight into the drivers that motivate people, you can begin to observe potential threats to yourself or the group. Going back to the reason you joined a group in the first place, there is safety in numbers. Initially in the slow burn scenario, there will be plenty of interaction time with the general public. As time progresses, assuming a slow event such as economic depression, the spread between the haves and the have-nots will become greater. Petty crime will increase, assaults, burglaries, etc. will become more prevalent. Law enforcement will be forced to crack down on everybody. This situation will only become worse as the bad guys give the good guys a reason to come down even harder. This cycle will continue as the citizenry demands further protection. During this period you will want to practice your situational awareness to reduce your chances of becoming a victim.

If the societal situation deteriorates to the point where the group activates, you will want to increase your defensive posture. As a note, there may be times prior to activation that it will be prudent to increase security through additional awareness and active measures. Anytime you have full group activation at the retreat location, you will want to provide around the clock security. We won't get too deep into the details of every scenario but we will cover the basics and a little more here.

Increased Situational Awareness

Sometimes we go places where we stay a little more alert to our surroundings. Think of a dark parking lot as opposed to a well-lit public place. That increase in looking behind you and avoiding blind spots is commonly referred to as situational awareness.

Now let's inject that scenario into a devolving society where maybe the nation's trucks stop running and stores are empty due to a pandemic. People everywhere are starving and out of work. All of a sudden walking through that dark parking lot sounds like an even worse idea. By ratcheting up your awareness, you might think twice before going out at night at all let alone strolling through a dark parking lot. You have now increased your security by choosing to avoid potential confrontations just by becoming more aware.

Now let's take it a little further. Our pandemic scenario has settled in. There are rolling brown outs due to a high number of workers staying home. Services have all but shut down. Food is running out for large numbers of people and city water is no longer dependable.

Does this qualify as a good time to activate the group? Possibly, but members may be trapped in their neighborhoods due to travel restrictions (The government calls this *Containment Operations*). What kind of security does your situation call for now that you are stuck in place? At this time you should have already increased your security to a rotating watch cycle, you have assessed your neighborhood for increased trouble and you have looked at your own home from all angles including the street view to see what image you are presenting.

Another reason for this is to detect approaches, blind spots and weaknesses. Hopefully you have enough people to provide such security. All the while you are planning your escape to join the group (assuming of course that you or anyone with you is not a carrier of the illness).

Security Activation At The Retreat

Lets flip the coin and say that the group has activated and most members have arrived. Your security plan will vary somewhat depending on whether the retreat location is urban or rural. Actually there will be many factors that come into play when planning and manning a security operation. Yes, it will be an operation. Anything that requires ongoing attention at all hours of the day and night can be considered an operation. Whether you are rural or urban, you have one primary goal, to provide for the health and welfare of the people under your umbrella. While the mission is simple in definition, it is not always so simple in application.

From a security perspective, the retreat location should have had a hazard analysis as we described earlier.

In that analysis the entire perimeter should have been walked and tested for vulnerability. Be sure to include the structure. To properly understand entry points and vulnerabilities, look at everything from the aggressor's perspective. Don't cheat yourself and don't underestimate the ingenuity of others. If you are going to take survival seriously you need to make sure your security is up to snuff.

Be warned that not all threats begin with an all-out assault.

Some problems begin with a knock on the door.

Chapter 18

MAKING DUE THROUGH BASELINE PREPAREDNESS

"The only real security that a man can have in this world is a reserve of knowledge, experience and ability."
                                                            Henry Ford

The ideal situation is a moving target. The survivalist must be patient and not expect too much, too soon. This goes for each member of the group. Flexibility, versatility, adaptability and resourcefulness are important factors in any disruptive situation. The best recipe for success of any survival situation is to be prepared as much as possible. In many cases preparedness falls back on knowledge more than materials.

We have laid out a number of things that can and will go wrong with a survival group. We have also offered a number of specific solutions to those problems, but perhaps the most important thing we can do is attempt to attract similarly interested, quality members. Beyond this, the next step is to promote individual readiness. The group will work better if everyone participates and contributes evenly.

We mentioned *baseline preparedness* but what does that mean in real terms? It means that based on a specific period of time, the members of a family are able to sustain themselves without assistance.

At the very least anyone interested in the pursuit of their own survival should take stock of their situation and strengthen the weak areas.

Start by selecting a period of time that you feel comfortable in preparing for. Don't overwhelm yourself right out of the gate. If this is new to you begin by taking stock of what you already have and go from there. Work evenly and methodically in the areas we have already discussed. Start simple and be able to sustain yourself and family for 3 days then advance to 2 weeks, then 30 days, 3 months, 6 months and so on.

Survival is not only about food. Try to work in a way that prepares you medically, safely and provides for the basic human needs. Become knowledgeable about the world around you and learn ways to minimize the hazards and disruptions that can affect you. Be mobile as soon as possible and never pass an opportunity to learn something. Most of all don't forget why you read this book in the first place. To build relationships with those who will support you in the journey of survival.

I hope that you have found this text useful in your survival planning. There are always more questions than answers with the unknown. The best we can do is think, learn, plan and act when necessary.

"The possession of knowledge does not kill the sense of wonder and mystery. There is always more mystery."

Anais Nin

ABOUT THE AUTHOR

Charley Hogwood served 15+ years in the U.S. Army and the Florida National Guard. Trained as a reconnaissance scout his experience covers a wide range of specialties from tactical environments to Radiological/Chemical situations to complex human disasters

As Chief Instructor and Executive Director for P.R.E.P. Personal Readiness Education Programs, LLC, Charley is responsible for designing and teaching over 40 different courses in various areas of emergency preparedness and disaster readiness, as well as urban and wilderness survival. Currently he is pursuing a degree in Emergency Management to add to his extensive skill set.

Charley also speaks at various preparedness events and provides private consultations to individuals, survival groups and other organizations on preparedness and leadership.

He lives near the Florida Everglades Swamp with the love of his life, wonderful daughter and his Brazilian Mastiff, Rufus, who chips away at his sanity daily.

Additional information on prepping/survival/groups and leadership can be seen at **www.readygoprep.com**

Appendix A

Glossary

3-Monthers
Seemingly good candidates who start out strong but self-destruct after about 3 months

AAR
After Action Review / Report

Activation
The calling together of the group for a specific reason

Active Defense
Obvious, aggressive security measures.

Agenda
Meeting discussion topics

All Hazards Approach
A method that understands that many different types of emergencies have similarities, Responses will be similar. This reduces the assets and skills required.

Annex
Annexes provide instructions for specific operations. Reduces the need to be specific in a plan. Just refer to an existing annex.

Attrition
Loss of supplies or personnel over time

Background Check
A criminal check of an individual's background

Bartering
Trading of items in place of currency

Baseline Preparedness
Minimum levels of supplies and basic skills

Baseline Requirements
Established minimum levels of supplies and skills

Behavioral Mimicry
Used to describe the behavior that people display when in numbers. Mimicking of another's behavior to gain status in a relationship

Blind Spot
An unknown condition; an area behind an obstacle; ignoring facts because you cannot relate to the situation

Brevity
Being brief, using fewer words to communicate

Bug-Out
Evacuating a location

Call Tree
Telephone roster broken into teams using Span of Control

CERT
Community Emergency Response Team, A federally funded program to prepare citizen teams to respond to disaster in their communities

Charity
Offering assistance to those in need

Cliques
Closed groups of people with similar interests who don't usually let others in

Collective Task
A task that requires multiple people to accomplish

Commerce
Buying, selling, bartering

Communication
Imparting or exchanging of information

Consensus
A general agreement among participants

Constitution
A body of fundamentals to which an organization is acknowledged to be governed; Supreme laws

Contingencies
A future event or circumstance that is possible but cannot be predicted with certainty, things to plan for

CTX
Classroom Training Exercise

Decision Making
A process used to develop plans and actions

Diversity
Variety

Energy Resources
Firewood, alternative power materials

EOC
Emergency Operations Center

Exercises
A task or activity done to practice or test a skill.

Food Insecurity
Not knowing where your next meal will come from; not receiving daily requirement of nutrients, malnourished

Food Production
The act of producing foods by growing and harvesting, animal harvesting

Food Storage
Creating a surplus of food and thoughtfully storing for the future based on needs and nutritional requirements

Foraging
Searching for food, collecting wild edibles

FTX
Field Training Exercise

Gap
A space in a plan where the dots do not connect; a missing domino in a sequence, which may collapse a plan

Gap Analysis
Testing and validating of plans to ensure that each action will support another required action

Group Dynamics
The processes involved when people in a group interact with each other

Group Efficacy
The ability of a group to accomplish its goals

Group Fragmentation
When members of a group splinter due to differing views, values and goals. Sometimes the action causes remaining members to take sides or polarize

Hazard
A potential source of danger

Hazard Analysis
Methodically searching out and prioritizing potential dangers based on vulnerability and risk

Hazard Tree
An exercise used to play out the possible events that a hazard may cause to reveal blind spots in a plan or additional hazards

HOA
Home Owner's Association

Hybrid Tree
An exercise similar to the hazard tree with the inclusion of responses to reveal gaps in planning, equipment and skills

Impact
The effect or influence a hazard may have on people, structures or processes

Impact Analysis
Considers the probable outcome of the event as it relates to you. How could this hazard impact your life?

Independence Conflict
When self-reliant, independent people give up some of their independence in order to join a group, understanding that the group comes first in most decisions

Individual Task
A task that is performed by a single person. The task may also be a part of a collective task.

Location Security
The combination of a workable security plan, adequate physical security and defendable terrain

Mission Statement
A statement that defines who your group is and how you want to operate

Mob Mentality
When multiples of people get together and act poorly because the group provides a level of anonymity, which allows people to do things, they would normally not do with little risk of being caught. Infectious bad behavior

Mobility
The ability to be mobile; Can be measured if desired with a mobility factor. Useful to get a consensus of how mobile the group is in certain conditions

Morale
The confidence, enthusiasm and discipline of a person or group at a specific time

Multiplication Factor
When a member brings unaccounted for people to the group or people fail to arrive. The group can figure approximately a +/-10% factor for the purposes of storing extra supplies as a contingency

Mutiny
An open rebellion against authority

Mutual Aid
Pledging to come to the aid of each other as individuals

Mutual Aid Compact
Groups pledging to come to the aid of each other

Mutual Assistance Group
A number of people who pledge to assist each other in times of trouble; usually trains regularly and seeks to attract members with similar values and relevant skills

Normalcy Bias
The feeling that nothing bad will happen and there is no reason to worry. If it does, help will come soon

Oath
A solemn promise regarding one's future action or behavior

OP/LP
Observation Post/Listening Post, a manned position usually deployed out front of a perimeter to provide advance warning of enemy activity in the area

Passive Defense
Unobtrusive security measures. Giving the appearance that little security is present. Also, waiting for an attack to happen before anything is done about it

Plan
A detailed proposal for doing or achieving something

Priorities Of Work
The tasking of duties based on what is most important at the time

QRF
Quick Reaction Force. A special rotating security contingent that is always ready to respond to danger or attack. Usually hidden in the center of a compound out of site and not deployed until absolutely necessary for fear of disclosing the true capabilities of a group in a probing attack

Refugee
A person who has been forced to leave their location to escape danger. Often with few if any supplies

Resource
A stock or supply of money, materials, people or other assets to draw on in order to function

Retreat
A fallback location where everyone meets in case of disaster. Usually a building that can provide shelter and protection as well as storage for pre-positioned supplies

Retreat Group
A loosely based group of people who will meet at the retreat location in case of disaster to support each other and provide mutual assistance

Risk
The level of probability that a hazard will affect you; the chances of something happening

Risk Assessment
A matrix that calculates the chances of certain known hazards at a particular location

Risk Homeostasis
Accepting a calculated level of danger based on perceptions and confidence then modifying the behavior to act with a lesser regard for one's safety. Ignoring warnings

ROE
Rules Of Engagement; Specific conditions under which force may be projected

Shelter Resources
Building materials, wilderness sheltering materials

SHTF
Sh*t Hits The Fan. Meaning bad things happen, from chaos to possibly a systemic collapse of society

SITREP
Situational Report; what is happening and what is your status

Situational Awareness
Being aware of your surroundings, looking out for trouble

Social Conflict
The struggle for power in a group or society. When two or more actors oppose each other in social interaction to prevent each other from having resources or power

Spoiler Attack
Attacking someone else before they attack you or to make others fight so that they leave you alone

Stray Cat Syndrome
Happens when you feed someone then they keep coming back for more. Others may hear about it and also come looking for handouts. Could lead to an attack

Strip Map
A simple hand drawn map depicting a target location and shows avenues of approach from each direction. Includes landmarks, target address and direction of North

Surplus
More than immediately needed

Survival Group
A group of people who meet and train together regularly in the ways of survival and self-reliance

Survivor
A person who has chosen to plan in advance for disastrous events and learn skills useful in the ways of survival. One who has survived a disastrous event

Synergy
The cooperation of two or more organizations or people to produce a combined effect greater than the sum of their separate effects

Tactical Perimeter
A physical ring of security around one's location. Usually in three layers

Team Charter
A document that defines what the purpose of the team is, how organized and what is expected of them

Team Conflict
Disagreement or power struggle within a team to the point the team is not effective

Training Compact
An agreement with another group or organization to provide training opportunities to each other's members

Transient Traffic
People or vehicles that are passing through an area on the way to somewhere else.

Trigger Points
An event that triggers another or a series of events that may have profound effects on our lives. The first domino to fall

Vetting
A careful and critical examination of someone. Usually conducted before trusting them with a position of responsibility

Vulnerability
How susceptible you are to a hazard

Water Resources
Sources of useful water in quantity

Appendix B

Rule of Threes For Survival

In An Emergency: Apply the Basic Rule of Threes

- 3 Minutes without air
- 3 hours without shelter
- 3 Days without water
- 3 Weeks without food

Based on your situation, these are the limits of time before one may be significantly impaired or perish.

Cognitive and physical decline will begin sooner than you think so don't wait until you count to three to improve one of these categories.

Appendix C
Sample Commo Plan
Out of Area Contact

Name _____

Phone Number _____

Address _____

Where is the overall map?

_____

Where is the strip map?

_____

Local Contact

Name _____

Phone Number _____

Address _____

Where is the overall map?

_____

Where is the strip map?

_____

Neighbourhood Rally Point

_____

Strip Map? Yes ☐   No ☐

Contact information _____

Local Rally Point

_____

Strip Map? Yes ☐   No ☐

Contact information _____

Regional Rally Point

_____

Strip Map? Yes ☐   No ☐

Contact information _____

Message Drops

_____

Strip Map? Yes ☐   No ☐

Contact information _____

Alternate Message Drops

_____

Strip Map? Yes ☐   No ☐

Contact information _____

Ham Radio

Primary Frequency_____

Contact call sign_____

Alternate Freqs:

Time of day the station is monitored:

Alternate Call Signs:

_____

_____

CB Radio Channels:

_____

Switch channel code word: _____

Walkie Talkie Channels:

_____

Switch Channel Code Word: _____

Appendix D

Decision Making / Problem Solving Process

In An Emergency:
- o Identify the problem
- o Identify options available for success
- o Select and apply the best option available
- o If no success, reevaluate and select new options until success is achieved

Right or wrong, you must make a decision; your gut will usually know right away what to do.

==

In A Non-Emergency:
- o Specify what exactly the decision/problem is
- o Determine who needs to be involved
- o What is best for the group goals
- o Apply problem solving format
    - o *Identify the problem*
    - o *Identify options available for success*
    - o *Select and apply the best option available*
    - o *If no success, reevaluate and select new options until success is achieved*

Verify The Decision process
- o Is there a blind spot or bias in the decision?
    - o Was mind open to all solutions?
    - o Was pride or prejudice involved?
    - o Does everyone understand the problem?
- o Is there a gap in the final decision?
    - o Will every step support the next step?
    - o Do you have the tools, people, skills and equipment to perform the operation?
    - o Does everyone understand his or her role?
    - o Are all players on board?

Don't fall victim to paralysis by analysis decide!

Appendix E

Quick Reference Guide: Forming a Group

- Prepare yourself
    - Define your reasons
    - Define your goals and values
    - Who are you responsible for?
    - Your hazard analysis
    - Where would you want to be in a long term event
    - Work your plan
- Look for others
    - Define what you are looking for from others
    - Refer to chapter 1 for places to find others
    - Begin speaking to others
    - Maintain privacy for both sides
    - Form alliances
- Organize
    - Schedule meetings
    - Set group values
    - Build foundation
    - Select leadership model
    - Define roles
- Maintain
    - Group team building exercises
    - Training sessions
    - Classes
    - Social events
    - Maintain/improve morale
    - Drills for readiness
    - Perform daily activities
- Correct dysfunction
    - Improve communication
    - Reestablish roles
    - Remove problem members

- Add members
  - Communicate group goals
  - Interview and vet candidates
  - Get member off to a good start
  - Keep them interested
- Understand surroundings
  - Link up with community
  - Link up with other groups
  - Establish positive image
  - Establish commerce as needed
  - Recognize threats
- Manage threats
  - Gather Intel
  - Observe and control threats
  - Activate group as needed
  - Shelter in place
  - Evacuate as needed
  - Maintain secure profile

Appendix F

Quick Reference Guide: Picking a Survival Location In A Hurry

When looking for a place to stay think of the following considerations. How long do you need to stay there?

- Accessibility
- Defendability
- Concealment
- Cover
- Transient Traffic
- Shelter
- Food Resources
- Water Resources
- Health and Safety
- Energy Resources
- Communication
- Avenues of escape

Location Notes:

Appendix E
Reference materials

Army, U.S. "Human Factor Considerations of Undergrounds in Insurgencies." <u>Department of the Army Pamphlet</u>. Department of the Army, Setember 1966.

Army, U.S. <u>Ranger Handbook</u>. Fort Benning: United States Army Infantry School Ranger Training Brigade, 1992.

Auf der Heide, Erik. <u>Disaster Response: Principles of Preparation and Coordination.</u> Online Textbook. http://www.coe-dmha.org/Media/Disaster_Response_Principals.pdf

Baggetta, Matthew et al. "Leading Associations: How Individual Characteristics and Team Dynamics Generate Committed Leaders." <u>American Sociological Review</u> XX.X (2013): 1-30.

Beheshtifar, Malikeh and Zare, Elham. "Interpersonal Conflict: A Substantial Factor to Organizational Failure." <u>International Journal of Academic Research in Business and Social Sciences</u> 3.5 (2013): 400-407.

Brymer, Melissa et al. <u>Psychological First Aid: Field Operations Guide</u>. National Child Traumatic Stress Network and National Center for PTSD, 2005.

Conflict Competence. www.conflictcompetence.com

Corgnet, Brice. "Peer Evaluations and Team Performance: When Friends Do Worse Than Strangers." Economic Inquiry 50.1 (2012): 171-181.

Downs, William D. Stories of Survival: Arkansas Farmers During the Great Depression. Fayetteville: Phoenix International Inc., 2011.

Erickson, Paul. Emergency Response Planning for Corporate and Municipal Managers. Burlington: Elsevier Butterworth-Heinemann, 2006.

Ferris, Kerry and Stein, Jill. The Real World: An Introduction to Sociology. 3d edition. New York: W.W. Norton and Co., 2012

Friedman, Ron. "Motivation is Contagious." Psychology Today (2013): 50-51.

Golec de Zavala, Agnieszka et al. "Collective Narcissism Moderates the Effect of In-Group Image Threat on Intergroup Hostility." Journal of Personality and Social Psychology 104.6 (2013): 1019-1039.

Holderman, Eric. How You Can Lead Without Authority (Opinion). Emergency Management: Strategy and Leadership in Critical Times.
http://www.emergencymgmt.com/training/Lead-Without-Authority-Opinion.html

Kayastha, Christina. The Discussion Facilitator - How One Member Alters Group Dynamics. Rochester: University of Rochester, 2012.

Kendall, Diana. Social Problems in a Diverse Society. 6th edition. Upper Saddle River: Pearson, 2013

Lucas, Jeffrey. "Behavioral and Emotional Outcomes of Leadership in Task Groups." Social Forces 78.2 (1999): 747-776.

Mind Tools. Golden Rules of Goal Setting: Five Rules to Set Yourself Up For Success.
http://www.mindtools.com/pages/article/newHTE_90.htm

Mind Tools. Helping Your People Find Purpose in Their Work: Finding Deeper Meaning in a Job.
http://www.mindtools.com/pages/article/find-purpose-work.htm#np

Mind Tools. Improving Group Dynamics: Helping Your Team Work More Effectively.
http://www.mindtools.com/pages/article/improving-group-dynamics.htm#np

Mind Tools. Leading Equals: Motivating People Effectively, Without Authority.
http://www.mindtools.com/pages/article/newLDR_64.htm#np

Mind Tools. Organizing Team Decision Making: Reaching Consensus for Better Decisions.
http://www.mindtools.com/pages/article/newTED_86.htm#np

Mind Tools. Resolving Team Conflict: Building Stronger Teams by Facing Your Differences.
http://www.mindtools.com/pages/article/newTMM_79.htm

Mind Tools. Successful Induction: Getting New Team Members Off To A Great Start.
http://www.mindtools.com/pages/article/newHTE_90.htm

Mind Tools. Team Charters: Getting Your Team Off To a Great Start.
http://www.mindtools.com/pages/article/newTMM_95.htm

Sibthorp, Jim et al. "Exploring Participant Developtment Through Adventure-Based Programming: A Model from the National Outdoor Leadership School." Leisure Sciences 29 (2007): 1-17.

University of Technology Sydney. Getting Groups Started. Online Article.
http://www.iml.uts.edu.au/learn-teach/groupwork/unit4.html

Vacharkulksemsuk, Tanya and Fredrickson, Barbara L. "Strangers in Sync: Achieving embodied rapport through shared movements." Journal of Experimental Social Psychology 48 (2012): 399-402.

Wilde, Gerald J.S. Target Risk. New York: PDE Publications, 1994.

Zimbardo, P.G. "A Situationist Perspective on the Psychology of Evil: Understanding How Good People Are Transformed Into Perpetrators." (Ed), A.G. Miller. The Social Psychology of Good and Evil. New York: Guilford Press, 2004. 21-50.

Zimbardo, Phillip. The Lucifer Effect: Understanding How Good People Turn Evil. New York: Random House, 2007

INDEX

3

3-monthers · 66

A

AAR · 133, 163
activation · 26, 27, 29, 41, 81, 91, 97, 139, 152, 167, 168, 169, 170, 173, 174, 175, 177, 178, 196, 197, 221, 244, 245
Active Defense · 108, 109
agenda · 111, 146, 177, 183, 184, 185
All Hazards Approach · 143, 145
Annex · 153
attrition · 54, 64

B

background check · 119, 207
Bartering · 213, 215, 218, 219, 220, 221
BASELINE PREPAREDNESS · 247
baseline requirements · 195, 196
Behavioral Mimicry · 238
blind spot · 100, 161, 163, 164, 166
blind spots · 100, 142, 146, 185, 244, 245
Brevity · 56, 120
bug-out · 20, 29, 168, 169, 198, 199

C

Call Tree · 177, 178, 179
CERT · 20
charity · 142, 221, 222
Cliques · 67, 135
collective task · 32, 39, 53, 80, 91, 107, 181
commerce · 64, 89, 90, 225, 228, 233
communication · 33, 36, 37, 60, 83, 89, 90, 94, 99, 112, 120, 126, 128, 129, 134, 137, 167, 168, 170, 174, 176, 177, 178, 179, 181, 184, 186, 199, 200
Communications · 120
Consensus · 34, 38, 42, 43, 75, 161
Constitution · 42, 43, 55, 60, 61, 62
constitutional · 61
constitutions · 61
CONTINGENCIES · 139, 141, 152, 165, 174, 176, 227

D

DECISION MAKING · 31, 67, 159, 161, 165
DIVERSITY · 112, 193

E

Energy Resources · 83, 89
EOC · 20
exercises · 125, 126, 128, 129, 130, 131, 132, 138, 212

F

Food insecurity · 240
food production · 40, 83, 86, 104, 116, 192
food storage · 50, 210
Foraging · 104, 106, 116

G

Gap · 94, 100, 112, 133, 146, 161, 162, 163, 164, 178, 185, 236
Gap Analysis · 161
group dynamics · 13, 24, 95, 133
Group Efficacy · 70
group fragmentation · 45, 68

H

hazard · 85, 88, 139, 140, 141, 142, 143, 145, 146, 151, 156, 235, 245
Hazard Analysis · 140
Hazard Tree · 142, 143
HOA · 66, 67
Hybrid Tree · 146

I

Impact · 140
Impact Analysis · 140
Independence Conflict · 25, 39, 43, 56
individual task · 91, 107

L

Location Security · 84

M

mission statement · 28, 51, 52, 53, 54, 56, 57, 193
mob mentality · 67, 239
mobility · 89, 198
morale · 35, 67, 70, 73, 83, 101, 105, 113, 121, 123, 131, 133
Multiplication Factor · 24
mutiny · 45, 54, 64, 187
Mutual Aid · 226, 228, 233
Mutual Aid Compact · 226, 233
Mutual Assistance Group · 15, 27

N

Normalcy Bias · 96, 97

O

Oath · 56, 57, 58, 212
OP/LP · 102

P

Passive Defense · 108
Plan · i, 51, 93, 139, 150, 151, 152, 153, 154, 155, 164, 173, 175, 179, 221

Q

QRF · 102, 155

R

refugee · 59, 81, 124, 208
resource · 63, 87, 89, 98, 113, 213, 215, 216, 217, 222, 225

retreat · 19, 28, 29, 32, 49, 79, 81, 82, 84, 98, 105, 108, 162, 169, 174, 175, 176, 195, 196, 198, 199, 200, 208, 243, 244, 245
Retreat Group · 79, 81
Risk · 140, 236, 238
Risk Homeostasis · 236
ROE · 64, 113

S

Shelter Resources · 83, 88
SHTF · 16, 17
SITREP · 98, 99, 116
situational awareness · 109, 243, 244
SOCIAL CONFLICT · 65
Stray Cat Syndrome · 221
strip map · 170, 172
surplus · 124, 213, 218, 219, 220, 221
SURVIVAL GROUP · 23, 25, 48, 65, 67, 75, 79, 81, 83, 91, 100, 103, 117, 127, 128, 139, 167, 176, 187, 189, 190, 194, 198, 203, 211, 213, 218, 227, 239, 241, 247

survivor · 13, 30, 61, 79, 81, 86, 111, 117, 123, 159, 163, 198, 235
synergy · 17, 68

T

Tactical Perimeter · 243
Team Charter · 109, 110, 131
Training Compact · 234
Transient traffic · 85
Trigger Points · 148, 149

V

VETTING · 30, 60, 187, 201
vulnerability · 84, 98, 140, 246

W

Water Resources · 83, 87

Taking you from reactive to proactive based on years of military, personal and professional experience with natural and man-made emergency situations.

Check out all of our social media to stay in touch!

www.facebook.com/readygoprep

www.twitter.com/shoestringprep

www.pinterest.com/readygoprep

www.youtube.com/readygoprep

www.readygoprep.com

MAGS: The People Part Of Prepping

IT'S THE DIGITAL AGE
YOUR BUSINESS/ORGANIZATION/GROUP NEEDS AN ONLINE PRESENCE

Website Design & Development
— and Information Technology Consulting/Support —

Our robust development platforms...

PROMIGEN^SM **PROMIFLEX**^SM

...are built on the solid WordPress System Architecture

View Our Website Development Portfolio at
www.DigitalProminence.com

NOTES

NOTES

NOTES

NOTES

NOTES

NOTES

NOTES

NOTES

NOTES

Made in the USA
Coppell, TX
13 February 2022

73523632R00167